At Issue

Will the World Run Out of Fresh Water?

Other Books in the At Issue Series:

At Issue

Will the World Run Out of Fresh Water?

David Haugen and Susan Musser, Book Editors

GREENHAVEN PRESS
A part of Gale, Cengage Learning

 GALE
CENGAGE Learning·

Detroit • New York • San Francisco • New Haven, Conn • Waterville, Maine • London

Elizabeth Des Chenes, *Managing Editor*

© 2012 Greenhaven Press, a part of Gale, Cengage Learning.

Gale and Greenhaven Press are registered trademarks used herein under license.

For more information, contact:
Greenhaven Press
27500 Drake Rd.
Farmington Hills, MI 48331-3535
Or you can visit our Internet site at gale.cengage.com

For product information and technology assistance, contact us at

Gale Customer Support, 1-800-877-4253
For permission to use material from this text or product, submit all requests online at www.cengage.com/permissions.

Further permissions questions can be e-mailed to permissionrequest@cengage.com.

Articles in Greenhaven Press anthologies are often edited for length to meet page requirements. In addition, original titles of these works are changed to clearly present the main thesis and to explicitly indicate the author's opinion. Every effort is made to ensure that Greenhaven Press accurately reflects the original intent of the authors. Every effort has been made to trace the owners of copyrighted material.

Cover photograph copyright Debra Hughes, 2007. Used under license from Shutterstock .com.

LIBRARY OF CONGRESS CATALOGING-IN-PUBLICATION DATA

Will the world run out of fresh water? / David Haugen and Susan Musser, book editors.
    p. cm. -- (At issue)
  Includes bibliographical references and index.
  ISBN 978-0-7377-5608-1 -- ISBN 978-0-7377-5609-8
  1. Water supply. 2. Water consumption. 3. Water resources development. I. Haugen, David M., 1969- II. Musser, Susan.
  TD345.W55 2011
  333.91--dc23
                                       2011042697

Printed in the United States of America
1 2 3 4 5   16 15 14 13 12

FD069

Contents

Introduction

Only 2.5 to 3 percent of all the natural water sources available on earth are composed of fresh water. Of that small percentage, less than 1 percent is easily accessible for human use; most of the rest is locked up in polar ice caps or buried deep in underground aquifers that catch and hold groundwater. For this reason, it is clear why human settlements have, for millennia, arisen chiefly near rivers and lakes and why irrigation was such a significant innovation for the growth and expansion of civilizations. Fresh water has always been a necessity for human life. It is an essential nutrient both for hydration and for growing sustainable food crops, and, like air, it is an element that no one can go long without.

It is difficult to believe, then, that such a precious resource may be dwindling through careless exploitation. Environmentalists and politicians have warned that a lack of education about the importance of fresh water has led to both overuse and defilement of the planet's fresh water sources. In 1997, the United Nations (UN) and the Stockholm Environment Institute told the UN Earth Summit Review Board that pollution and uncontrolled consumption were the chief threats to the world's fresh water. More than a decade later, those threats have not changed. A white paper released by Veolia Water and the International Food Policy Research Institute in 2010 highlights that, because of irresponsible human use, "the functioning and quality of watersheds and irrigated lands are deteriorating, and ground and surface water pollution is increasing."

The chief culprits of freshwater use and pollution are agriculture and industry. According to the US Department of Agriculture, irrigation and other agricultural projects consume 80 percent of consumptive (nonreturnable) fresh water used in the United States. The percentage is even higher in Asia. Globally, the percentage of fresh water used for agriculture is roughly 70 percent. Though watering cropland is a necessity, critics claim many current methods of irrigation are wasteful. The US Geological Survey contends that about half the water used in agriculture is lost through leaking transport pipes and through natural evaporation off the ground and crops. The remaining non-consumptive water is carried away as runoff that eventually soaks into groundwater repositories. Unfortunately, the runoff may contain chemicals and pesticides used to treat crops, thus tainting these groundwater resources. In developed nations like the United States, farmers are learning to capture runoff so it can be reused on crops. In developing nations, however, the expertise and infrastructure needed to employ such techniques may be lacking.

Industrial processes (including the making of paper, plastic, wood, and metal goods) and power plant cooling systems also consume fresh water. In the United States, about 4 percent of water withdrawals go to industries, according to the Geological Survey. Globally, industries consume more than 20 percent of fresh water used by humans. This water is commonly discharged back into surface water and groundwater ecosystems. In a January/February 2000 *World Watch* magazine article, Payal Sampat wrote, "In many parts of the developing world, factories still dump their liquid effluents onto the ground and wait for it to disappear. In the Bolivian city of Santa Cruz, for example, a shallow aquifer that is the city's main water source has had to soak up the brew of sulfates, nitrates, and chlorides dumped over it." In the United States, the Environmental Protection Agency sets high treatment standards for industrial discharge, but water runoff from construction sites, gas stations, and other businesses may often be overlooked as a source of pollutants.

In comparison to agriculture and industry, less than 10 percent of fresh water resources are consumed by households as drinking water. Given that agriculture, for example, will likely use more water as global populations grow, this small portion of drinking water will not get larger without significant conservation efforts or the tapping of new supplies (such as polar ice). Thus, concerned individuals fear that the world is heading for a water crisis in which supply cannot meet eventual demand. Writing in the 2010 issue of *Food Policy*, Munir A. Hanjra and M. Ejaz Qureshi state that "Data on water supply and demand are startling: about 450 million people in 29 countries face severe water shortages ...; about 20% more water than is now available will be needed to feed the additional three billion people by 2025 ...; [and] as much as two-thirds of the world population could be water-stressed by 2025." The year 2025 was chosen as a target date by the International Water Management Institute in their 1998 report that charted global water scarcity since 1990 and made predictions about its future. As Hanjra and Qureshi ominously point out, "The 2025 projections on water scarcity ... were reached in 2000."

Most of the dire predictions concerned developing nations, and the United Nations and other global bodies have focused their attention on regions where poverty is high and access to fresh water is limited. For example, lack of infrastructure and capital has forced much of Sub-Saharan Africa to contend with water shortages, and similar conditions face parts of Asia and South America. The Middle East has a very restricted access to fresh water, but oil revenues have helped it survive through the building of desalination plants that turn seawater into potable water. However, as populations in this region increase and oil supplies peak, experts caution that the situation could become critical, possibly leading to violence. "Tensions run high within this area of unequally distributed water resources, under stress even during periods of average precipitation," writes Harald D. Frederiksen in the Winter 2009 issue of *Middle East Policy*. "The control of water could be a devastating weapon in Middle East conflicts."

Even though water shortages are a major concern for international relations, very few armed conflicts have been fought over water. Instead, access rights to water have often helped neighboring nations find grounds for diplomacy. Such opportunity for negotiation highlights the significance of fresh water, but many observers contend that the more pressing problem for global water supplies is one that dominates attitudes in developed nations. That is, the people in countries with vast freshwater delivery systems tend to forget about access and simply expect their taps to keep flowing. As Ran Sanghera writes in the *Financial Times* online on March 27, 2011, the true misfortune in the developed world is that "despite its critical importance to life on earth, water is taken for granted and the impending issue of water scarcity remains largely invisible and neglected."

The viewpoints collected in *At Issue: Will the World Run Out of Fresh Water?* however, reveal that the issue is not wholly neglected. Environmentalists, scientists, and other commentators provide their opinions on the state of fresh water access and use throughout the globe. While no one argues that the world will run out of fresh water, these authors show concern about how water is apportioned worldwide, how much fresh water is wasted, and whether solutions to the predicted crisis will be effective enough to alleviate expected shortages. Only by making these problems known and facing the challenges head-on can the global community hope to provide enough of this vital element to the roughly eight billion people expected to populate the earth within the next ten to fifteen years.

1

There Is a Looming Global Fresh Water Shortage

Paul Alois

Paul Alois is currently a doctoral student in international affairs at the City University of New York. He has previously worked as a researcher and writer for the World Bank and the Arlington Institute, a nonprofit think tank that examines national security in light of various forces of global change.

Water shortages have always plagued humanity, but in the modern age, the potential for serious depletions of fresh water reserves are increasing. The global population is growing significantly, and more and more people are suffering from poor access to drinking water. The majority of the world's water is being utilized by industry and agriculture, leaving less than 10 percent for human consumption. While humanity can flourish on the water available, not enough is being conserved to ensure that present populations and future generations have enough to drink. Pollutants, agricultural waste, and a shared ignorance of the importance of conserving water are all leading to the depletion of fresh water supplies. Humanity must be made aware of the implications of degrading water stocks, and governments, farmers, and citizens in general must act to preserve fresh water for a sustainable future.

Water, simply put, makes the existence of the human race on this planet possible. With few exceptions, water has always been a natural resource that people take for granted. Today, the situation has changed.

The World Bank reports that 80 countries now have water shortages and 2 billion people lack access to clean water. More disturbingly, the World Health Organization has reported that 1 billion people lack enough water to simply meet their basic needs.

Population growth and groundwater depletion present the two most significant dangers to global water stability. In the last century, the human population has increased from 1.7 billion people to 6.6 billion people, while the total amount of potable water has slightly decreased. Much of the population growth and economic development experienced in the last fifty years has been supported by subterranean water reserves called groundwater. These nonrenewable reserves, an absolutely essential aspect of the modern world, are being consumed at an unsustainable rate.

Approximately 1,700 m3 of water exists for every person on the planet, an alarming low number.

The Present Supply of Water and Its Use

Humanity has approximately 11 trillion cubic meters of freshwater at its disposal. Groundwater aquifers contain over 95% of this water, while rain, rivers, and lakes make up the remaining 5%. Approximately 1,700 m3 [cubic meters] of water exists for every person on the planet, an alarming low number. According to the Water Stress Index, a region with less than 1,700 m3 per capita is considered "water stressed".

The global supply is not distributed evenly around the planet, nor is water equally available at all times throughout the year. Many areas of the world have seriously inadequate access to water, and many places with high annual averages experience alternating seasons of drought and monsoons.

Water usage differs highly between developing countries and developed ones. Developing countries use 90% of their water for agriculture, 5% for industry, and 5% for urban areas. Developed countries use 45% of their water for agriculture, 45% for industry, and 10% for urban areas.

In the last century water usage per person doubled, even as the total population tripled, creating a situation today where many areas of the world are consuming water at an unsustainable rate.

The industrial sector accounts for 22% of global water consumption; this number will grow in the coming decades as the developing world industrializes.

Demand for Water Is Rising

The agricultural sector, by far the largest consumer of freshwater resources, accounts for 70% global consumption. Irrigation consumes most of the water in the agricultural sector, and has become an integral part of modern civilization because of access to groundwater aquifers. Once farmers were freed from relying on rain to water their crops, highly efficient commercial farming became increasingly common. This innovation also underpinned the Green Revolution, which dramatically increased crop production throughout the third world in the 1960s. Unfortunately, water is being drawn from many of these aquifers faster than it is being replaced.

The industrial sector accounts for 22% of global water consumption; this number will grow in the coming decades as the developing world industrializes. The needs of industry tend to take precedence over agriculture for simple economic reasons. 1,000 tons of water will produce 1 ton of wheat, which is worth $200. 1,000 tons of water in the industrial sector, however, will generate $14,000 worth of goods. On a per ton basis, industry creates 70 times more wealth. Despite its economic benefits, intense water use by industry has led to serious pollution that is beginning to create problems worldwide.

The residential sector uses the remaining 8% of the total water supply. Although this sector only accounts for a small percentage of overall use, it always takes precedence over industry and agriculture. In the last fifty years the world's urban population has exploded, and by 2010 50% of the people on the planet will live in cities. In addition to the simple increase in population, per person consumption of water has risen. As more people begin utilizing modern luxuries like flush toilets, showers, and washing machines, the demand created by the residential sector will increase dramatically.

Pollution Poisoning Water Supplies

The companion of modernization has always been pollution. In developing countries that are just entering the industrial age, water pollution presents a serious problem. According to United Nations Environmental Program (UNEP), "in developing countries, rivers downstream from major cities are little cleaner than open sewers". The UNEP also reports that 1.2 billion people are being affected by polluted water, and that dirty water contributes to 15 million child deaths every year. In recent years, scientists have become aware of the problems involved with the contamination of groundwater. Aquifers move very slowly, so once they are polluted it takes decades or centuries for them to cleanse themselves.

Water pollution is reaching epic proportions. In the U.S. 40% of rivers and lakes are considered too polluted to support normal activities.

Food production contributes significantly to water contamination. When nitrogen fertilizer is applied to a field, the water runoff will contain excess amounts of nitrates. Nitrates have been shown to have a very harmful effect on plant and animal life, can cause miscarriages, and can harm infant development. The industrial livestock business also presents a serious danger to water systems. The disposal of vast amounts of animal feces destroys nearby ecosystems and is very hazardous to humans.

Water pollution is reaching epic proportions. In the U.S. 40% of rivers and lakes are considered too polluted to support normal activities. In China 80% of the rivers are so polluted that fish cannot survive in them. In Japan 30% of groundwater has been contaminated by industrial pollution. The Ganges River [in India], which supports around 500 million people, is considered one of the most polluted rivers in the world. And the list goes on . . .

Food Scarcity from Lack of Water

According to the International Food Policy Research Institute (IFPRI), if current water consumption trends continue, by 2025 the agricultural sector will experience serious water shortages. The IFPRI estimates that crop losses due to water scarcity could be as high as 350 million metric tons per year, slightly more than the entire crop yield of the U.S. This massive water crisis will be caused by water contamination, diverting water for industrial purposes, and the depletion of aquifers. Climate change may also play a part. The Himalayan glaciers, which feed the rivers that support billions of people, are shrinking in size every year. Their disappearance would cause a major humanitarian disaster.

The greatest danger to global food security comes from aquifer depletion. Aquifers are an essential source of water for food production, and they are being overdrawn in the western U.S., northern Iran, north-central China, India, Mexico, Australia, and numerous other locations. Additionally, many aquifers are contaminated each year by pollution and seawater intrusion.

Despite their importance, data on underground water reservoirs remains imprecise. There is little evidence regarding how many aquifers actually exist, and the depth of known aquifers is often a mystery. However, it is clear that water from these sources takes centuries to replenish, and that they are being consumed at a highly unsustainable rate.

Water as a Source of Conflict

According to the UNEP, there are 263 rivers in the world that either cross or mark international boundaries. The basins fed by these rivers account for 60% of the world's above ground freshwater. Of these 263 rivers, 158 have no international legislation, and many are the source of conflict.

Water has always been a central issue in the Arab-Israeli situation. [Former Israeli Prime Minister] Ariel Sharon once said the Six Days War actually began the day that Israel stopped Syria from diverting the Jordan River in 1964. Decades later, the Egyptian military came close to staging a coup against Egyptian president Anwar Sadat, who had proposed diverting some of the Nile's water to Israel as part of a peace plan.

> *While a global water crisis has the potential to tear international relations at the seams, it also has the potential to force the global community into a new spirit of cooperation.*

The Nile River, which runs through Ethiopia, Sudan, and Egypt, exemplifies the potential for future water conflicts. The banks of the Nile River support one of most densely populated areas on the planet. In the next fifty years the number of people dependant on the Nile could double, creating a serious water crisis in the region. The Nile is not governed by any multilateral treaties, and Egypt would not shrink from using military strength to guarantee its future access to water.

The potential for water conflicts are less likely outside the Middle East, but never the less there are many problematic areas. The Mekong River is the lifeblood of South East Asia, but it begins in one of the most water poor countries on Earth: China. The Indus River separates Pakistan and India, and aquifer depletion by Indian farmers has one of the highest rates in the world. U.S.-Mexican relations are already strained over water use on their mutual border. The Niger River basin in West-Central Africa runs through five countries. Surging populations coupled with decreasing rainfall in the region seriously threaten water security for millions of people.

Although the specter of international water wars can seem very real, in the last 50 years there have only been 7 conflicts over water outside the Middle East. While a global water crisis has the potential to tear international relations at the seams, it also has the potential to force the global community into a new spirit of cooperation.

Better Water Management and Less Consumption

The oceans contain 97% of the world's water. Desalination technology transforms the vast amount of salt water in the Earth's oceans into freshwater fit for human consumption. There are approximately 7,500 desalination plants in the world, 60% of which are in the Middle East. The global desalination industry has a capacity of approximately 28 million m3, less than 1% of global demand. Desalination is an expensive and energy intensive technology, and currently only wealthy countries with serious water shortages consider it a viable option. However, a recent innovation using nanotechnology has the potential to decrease the cost of desalination by 75%, making it a more viable option.

While irrigation accounts for approximately one third of all global water consumption, numerous studies have shown that approximately half of the water used in irrigation is lost through evaporation or seepage. Drip irrigation technology offers a far more water-efficient way of farming. Drip irrigation techniques involve using a series of pipes to distribute water in a very controlled manner. By using this method farmers have the ability to give their crops the exact amount of water needed. Despite its many benefits, drip irrigation is not being widely implemented. While the technology is not sophisticated or expensive, it is beyond the means of the poorest farmers who need it most. It is also not being used by many farmers in water-rich countries because the potential savings are less than the cost of implementing the technology.

In many countries water shortages are exacerbated or even caused by governmental mismanagement, political infighting, and outright corruption.

In many countries water shortages are exacerbated or even caused by governmental mismanagement, political infighting, and outright corruption. International organizations like the World Trade Organization (WTO) often suggest that privatization of water management services would alleviate many of these problems. It has been shown that privatizing utilities frequently increases efficiency, innovation, and maintenance. However, privatization rarely has an effect on corruption, and often disadvantages the poor.

Other technical solutions like rainwater capture, water-free toilets, and water reclamation offer people the possibility of effective conservation. Market-oriented solutions such as water tariffs, pricing groundwater, and increasing fines against industries that pollute could be adopted. There are also a number of viable trade solutions. Freshwater could be traded internationally by using pipelines and enormous plastic bags. Despite this plethora of potential solutions, there is no substitute for simply consuming less.

Working Toward a Sustainable Future

In the coming decades, water crises will likely become increasingly common. If the population continues to grow at a rate of 1 billion people every 15 years, the Earth's capacity to support human life will be severely strained. Population growth notwithstanding, the current supply of water is being degraded by pollution, overdrawing, and climate change. It is not too late to guarantee a safe supply of water for everyone alive today and for all future generations; although to do so would require an unprecedented level of international cooperation, trust, and compassion.

2

People Must Learn Not to Take Water for Granted

Charles Fishman

Charles Fishman is the author of The Wal-Mart Effect *and* The Big Thirst: The Secret Life and Turbulent Future of Water. *He is a three-time winner of the Gerald Loeb Award for business journalism and writes regularly for the magazine* Fast Company.

In the early 1900s—when cities began instituting clean water systems—people no longer had to concern themselves with where fresh water came from or how much of it they were using. One expected that turning on the tap would yield clean water. This attitude has stayed with most people in the developed world. Most Americans, for example, no longer think about how much water they use or how they might conserve it. Part of the problem is ignorance, but another part is the invisibility of the water system. People are not made to think about how water is delivered to their homes or how the supply of fresh water is dwindling. It is vital to undermine this lack of concern and make everyone aware of how important it is to treat fresh water as a valuable resource that needs to be preserved in light of potential water shortages.

Water is both mythic and real. It manages to be at once part of the mystery of life and part of the routine of life. We can use water to wash our dishes and our dogs and our cars without giving it a second thought, but few of us can resist simply standing and watching breakers crash on the beach. Water has all kinds of associations and connections, implications and suggestiveness. It also has an indispensable practicality.

Water is the most familiar substance in our lives. It is also unquestionably the most important substance in our lives. Water vapor is the insulation in our atmosphere that makes Earth a comfortable place for us to live. Water drives our weather and shapes our geography. Water is the lubricant that allows the continents themselves to move. Water is the secret ingredient of our fuel-hungry society. That new flat-screen TV, it turns out, needs not just a wall outlet and a cable connection but also its own water supply to get going. Who would have guessed?

Water is also the secret ingredient in the computer chips that make possible everything from MRI machines to Twitter accounts. Indeed, from blue jeans to iPhones, from Kleenex to basmati rice to the steel in your Toyota Prius, every product of modern life is awash in water. And water is, quite literally, everywhere. When you take a carton of milk from the refrigerator and set it on the table, within a minute or two the outside is covered in a film of condensation—water that has migrated almost instantly from the air of the kitchen to the cold surface of the milk carton.

Everything human beings do is, quite literally, a function of water.

Most People Do Not Understand Their Relationship to Water

Everything human beings do is, quite literally, a function of water, because every cell in our bodies is plumped full of it, and every cell is bathed in watery fluid. Blood is 83 percent water. Every heartbeat is mediated by chemicals in water;

when we gaze at a starry night sky, the cells in our eyes execute all their seeing functions in water; thinking about water requires neurons filled with water.

Given that water is both the most familiar substance in our lives, and the most important substance in our lives, the really astonishing thing is that most of us don't think of ourselves as having a relationship to water. It's perfectly natural to talk about our relationship to our car or our relationship to food, our relationship to alcohol, or money, or to God. But water has achieved an invisibility in our lives that is only more remarkable given how central it is.

Back in 1999, a team of researchers recorded 289,000 toilet flushes of Americans in twelve cities, from Seattle to Tampa. The researchers used electronic water-flow sensors to record not just toilet flushes but every "water event" in each of 1,188 homes for four weeks. Although the study cost less than $1 million, it is considered so detailed and so pioneering that it hasn't been duplicated in the decade since; the U.S. Environmental Protection Agency continues to cite it as the definitive look at how Americans use water at home.

The researchers measured everything we do with water at home—how many gallons a bath takes, how often the clothes washer runs, how much water the dishwasher uses, who has low-flow showerheads and who has regular, how many times we flush the toilet each day, and how many gallons of water each flush uses.

The study's overall conclusion can be summed up in four words: We like to flush.

For Americans, flushing the toilet is the main way we use water. We use more water flushing toilets than bathing or cooking or washing our hands, our dishes, or our clothes. When we think about the big ways we use water, flushing the toilet doesn't typically leap to mind. It's one of those unnoticed parts of our daily water use—our daily watermark—that turns out to be both startling and significant.

The largest single consumer of water in the United States, in fact, is virtually invisible. Every day, the nation's power plants use 201 billion gallons of water in the course of generating electricity. That isn't water used by hydroelectric plants—it's the water used by coal, gas, and nuclear power plants for cooling and to make steam.

One of every six gallons of water pumped into water mains by U.S. utilities simply leaks away, back into the ground.

Vital Water Leaking Away

Toilets and electric outlets may be stealthy consumers of water, but they at least serve vital functions. One of the largest daily consumers of water isn't a use at all. One of every six gallons of water pumped into water mains by U.S. utilities simply leaks away, back into the ground.

Sixteen percent of the water disappears from the pipes before it makes it to a home or business or factory. Every six days, U.S. water utilities lose an entire day's water. And that 16 percent U.S. loss rate isn't too bad—British utilities lose 19 percent of the water they pump; the French lose 26 percent. There is perhaps no better symbol of the golden age of water, of the carefree, almost cavalier, attitude that our abundance has fostered. We go to the trouble and expense to find city-size quantities of water, build dams, reservoirs, and tanks to store it and plants to treat it, then we pump it out to customers, only to let it dribble away before anyone can use it.

One of the hallmarks of the twentieth century, at least in the developed world, is that we have gradually been able to stop thinking about water. We use more of it than ever, we rely on it for purposes we not only never see but can hardly imagine, and we think about it not at all. It is a striking achievement. We used to build monuments—even temples—to

23

water. The aqueducts of the Roman Empire are marvels of engineering and soaringly elegant design. They were plumbing presented as civic achievement and as a tribute to the water itself. Today, water has drifted so far from civic celebration that many people visit the Roman aqueducts without any sense at all that they moved water, or how.

When People Began Taking Water for Granted

Many cities in the world are located where they are because of their proximity to water. For most of human history, in most settings, getting water was part of the daily routine; it was a constant part of our mental landscape. At the same time, humanity's relationship to its water supply was wary, because water often made people sick. That's why Poland Spring water was so popular in Boston and New York even a century ago—it was safe.

One hundred years ago, with the dawn of bacteriology, two things happened. Cities started aggressively separating their freshwater supplies from their sewage disposal, something they had been surprisingly slow to do. (Philadelphia is just one of many cities whose sewage system, a hundred years ago, emptied into a river upstream of the city water supply intakes from the same river.)

And water utilities discovered that basic sand filters and chlorination could clean and disinfect water supplies, all but assuring their safety. In the decade from 1905 to 1915, as dozens of water systems around the country installed filters and chlorination systems, we went through a water revolution that profoundly improved human life forever.

Between 1900 and 1940, mortality rates in the United States fell 40 percent. How much did clean water matter? Harvard economist David Cutler and Stanford professor of medicine Grant Miller conducted a remarkable analysis, published in 2005, teasing out the impact of the new water treatment methods on the most dramatic reduction in death rates in U.S. history. By 1936, they conclude, simple filtration and chlorination of city water supplies reduced overall mortality in U.S. cities by 13 percent. Clean water cut child mortality in half.

[The] first water revolution ushered in an era—the one we think we still live in—in which water was unlimited, free, and safe. And once it was unlimited, free, and safe, we could stop thinking about it.

Clean municipal water encouraged cities to grow, and it also encouraged the expansion of "mains water" during the twentieth century as the way most Americans got their water. (By 2005, only 14 percent of Americans still relied on wells or some other "self-supplied" water.) That first water revolution ushered in an era—the one we think we still live in—in which water was unlimited, free, and safe. And once it was unlimited, free, and safe, we could stop thinking about it.

The fact that it was unfailingly available "on demand" meant that we would use it more, even as we thought about it less.

Our very success with water ushered in not just a golden age of water, but a century-long era in which water became increasingly invisible. Our home water bills, which are less than half our monthly cable TV or cell phone bills, provide almost no insight into how much water we use, or how we use it—even if we study them.

The new class of micropollutants we are beginning to hear about—infinitesimal, almost molecular, traces of plastics, birth control pills, antidepressants—have literally been invisible even to chemists until very recently; you certainly can't tell if they're in your water by looking at it or drinking it. The impact of those micropollutants on our health, if any, may remain invisible for years—and may be almost impossible to predict or trace.

Even our emotional connections to water have become submerged and camouflaged—the ease with which water enters and leaves our lives allows us an indifference to our water supply. We are utterly ignorant of our own watermark, of the amount of water required to float us through the day, and we are utterly indifferent to the mark our daily life leaves on the water supply.

The last century has conditioned us to think that water is naturally abundant, safe, and cheap—that it should be, that it will be. We're in for a rude shock.

The End of a Golden Age

But the golden age of water is rapidly coming to an end. The last century has conditioned us to think that water is naturally abundant, safe, and cheap—that it should be, that it will be. We're in for a rude shock.

We are in the middle of a water crisis already, in the United States and around the world. The experts realize it (the Weather Channel already has a dedicated burning-orange logo for its drought reports), but even in areas with serious water problems, most people don't seem to understand. We are entering a new era of water scarcity—not just in traditionally dry or hard-pressed places like the U.S. Southwest and the Middle East, but in places we think of as water-wealthy, like Atlanta [Georgia] and Melbourne [Australia].

The world has 6.9 billion people. At least 1.1 billion of us don't have access to clean, safe drinking water—that's one out of six people in the world. Another 1.8 billion people don't have access to water in their homes or yard, but do have access within a kilometer. So at least 40 percent of the world either doesn't have good access to water, or has to walk to get it.

In the next fifteen years, by 2025, the world will add 1.2 billion people. By 2050, we will add 2.4 billion people. So between now and forty years from now, more new people will join the total population than were alive worldwide in 1900. They will be thirsty.

And then there is the unpredictability of climate change. Water availability is intensely weather- and climate-dependent, in both the developed world and the developing world. At one point in 2008, during the years-long drought across the southeastern United States, 80 percent of the residents of North Carolina were living under water-use restrictions.

The Las Vegas [Nevada] area has 2 million residents and 36 million visitors a year, and its water source in January 2011 was lower than it had been in any January going back to 1965. At that time, Las Vegas had about 200,000 residents; today, on a typical day, there are twice that many tourists in town.

Beyond population and climate change, the other huge and growing pressure on water supplies is economic development. China and India are modernizing at a whirling pace, and together those two countries account for one out of three people in the world. Economic development requires rivers full of water, not just because people want more secure and more abundant water as their incomes improve but because modern factories and businesses use such huge volumes of water.

Becoming Aware of the Invisible Water System

It is a mistake to think that big water issues are not manageable, however. One of the most startling, inspiring and least well-known examples involves the United States. The United States uses less water today than it did in 1980. Not in per capita terms, in absolute terms. Water use in the United States peaked in 1980, at 440 billion gallons a day for all purposes. Today, the country is using about 410 billion gallons of water a day.

That performance is amazing in many ways. Since 1980, the U.S. population has grown by 70 million people. And since 1980, the U.S. GDP [gross domestic product] in real terms has more than doubled. We use less water to create a $13 trillion economy today than we needed to create a $6 trillion economy then.

In fact, the most unsettling attitude we've begun to develop about water is a kind of disdain for the era we've just lived through. The very universal access that has been the core of our water philosophy for the last hundred years—the provision of clean, dependable tap water that created the golden age of water—that very principle has turned on its head.

[The invisibility of the water system] makes it difficult for people to understand the effort and money required to sustain a system that has been in place for decades, but has in fact been quietly corroding from decades of neglect.

The brilliant invisibility of our water system—the sources of water unknown to the people who use it, the pipes buried under pavement, the treatment plants anonymous and tucked away, the water service itself so reliable that even the reliability is a kind of invisibility—that invisibility has become the system's most significant vulnerability.

That invisibility makes it difficult for people to understand the effort and money required to sustain a system that has been in place for decades, but has in fact been quietly corroding from decades of neglect. Why should I pay higher taxes just to replace some old water pipes? I'll just drink bottled water if I don't like what comes out of the tap. It is almost as if tap water is regarded not with respect and appreciation but with a hint of condescension, even contempt.

Of course, you can't call [the bottled water brand] Dasani if your house catches on fire. We are in danger of allowing ourselves to imagine that since we've got FedEx, we don't also need the postal service. When universal, twenty-four-hour-a-day access to water starts to slip away, it becomes very hard to bring back. But sustaining it requires more than paying the monthly water bill. If we're going to be ready for a new era of water, we need to reclaim water from our superficial sense of it, we need to reclaim it from the clichés. We need to rediscover its true value, and also the serious commitment required to provide it. It is one of the ironies of our relationship to water that the moment it becomes unavailable, the moment it really disappears—that's when water becomes most urgently visible.

3

Desalination Is Part of the Solution to Fresh Water Shortages

McKinley Conway

A former scientist for the National Aeronautics and Space Administration (NASA), McKinley Conway is an engineer and founder of Conway Data Inc., a company specializing in geo-economics, the proper implementation of workers and resources for local, national, and international development projects.

While conservation is the first countermeasure to shortages of fresh water, many global communities simply cannot provide enough drinking water for their inhabitants. Desalination plants are an excellent solution to this problem. If governments support this technology, desalination operations will become cheaper and safer and can supply coastal areas—and even some inland regions—with fresh water. Many state and national governments are already investing in desalination projects as an effective method to meet current needs and guard against future shortages.

Desalination is likely to become one of the world's biggest industries. Growing communities and new industries must have dependable water supplies in order to prosper. If droughts, exhaustion of groundwater sources, decline of lake or river levels, or a combination of such factors threaten an area's water supply, site-seeking firms may look elsewhere, giving water-rich areas a competitive advantage.

Certainly, water conservation programs should come first as a strategy for regions facing water problems. Many jurisdictions are already imposing water-use limits. Other communities try drilling wells deeper and deeper until their aquifer is maxed out, or they propose to pipe water from distant streams. But such shortsighted strategies can do incalculable damage to the environment.

Desalting systems have long proven effective in Kuwait, Bahrain, Qatar, the United Arab Emirates, Oman, and Saudi Arabia.

Desalination Is a Better Solution

There is a better solution. Desalting systems have long proven effective in Kuwait, Bahrain, Qatar, the United Arab Emirates, Oman, and Saudi Arabia. Where once there were bleak villages on barren deserts there are now bright modern cities with tree-lined streets. There are homes with lush gardens. In the countryside there are productive farms.

The big desalting plant at Jubail, Saudi Arabia, is a model for the world. A pipeline carries a river of freshwater 200 miles inland to the capital city of Riyadh, and desalted seawater has given a large region an entirely new future filled with opportunities.

There are more than 7,000 desalination plants, mostly small ones, in operation worldwide. About two-thirds are located in the Middle East, and others are scattered across islands in the Caribbean and elsewhere. Aruba's high-tech water plant has for many years met the needs of a thriving tourist industry.

The largest plant in the United States is the pioneering $158-million project of the Tampa Bay Water agency [in Florida]. The project was let to contract in 1999 and after overcoming some technical problems in its early years is now performing well and causing no significant environmental problems. But no U.S. water agency has yet undertaken a really big project comparable to those found along the Arabian Gulf.

Challenges to Overcome

The first obstacle is cost: Today's desalting plants are multibillion-dollar projects, and it will take time for improving technology to bring the cost down. Timid government officials and politicians delay action for years, during which the cost of a plant and related distribution facilities may double or triple.

Fuel for desalination is a major challenge. Desalination plants in most nations don't have access to cheap oil as do plants in the Middle East. So planners of big new units in the western United States need to think of energy from wind and solar installations. Along the Florida coast, ocean energy could become important. The Gulf Stream is an enormous asset waiting to be used. Electric utilities that need cooling water may engage in joint ventures for such undertakings.

Timid government officials and politicians delay action for years, during which the cost of a plant and related distribution facilities may double or triple.

Location Is Important

Today, plans are under way in California for a seawater desalting plant to meet about one-half of the water requirements of Santa Barbara. A group that includes Bechtel [Corporation] and several utilities has proposed to build a desalting plant near San Diego to produce 100 million gallons per day of potable water. A private developer has built a small plant on Catalina Island. North of San Francisco, Marin County is considering a seawater unit.

Texas, meanwhile, has built a $2-million pilot plant at Brownsville to explore ideas for a $150-million installation planned for 2010.

Coastal states obviously have a big advantage in coping with future water needs, and many cities sit at the ocean's edge or nearby. Inland cities are likely to face bigger problems, and, sooner than we think, it will be necessary to build pipelines to some of them. Right now, Las Vegas is planning a $2-billion, 300-mile pipeline to bring water from rural northeast Nevada counties to the city.

Today, plans are under way in California for a seawater desalting plant to meet about one-half of the water requirements of Santa Barbara.

Booming Orlando, Florida, has been expecting to meet future water needs by piping water from the St. Johns and other rivers. However, this scheme is strongly opposed by ecologists. After the expensive environmental mistakes of the cross-Florida barge canal and manipulation of the Everglades, the state may be hesitant to approve any more drastic changes in natural flow patterns.

Thus, Orlando could be the first large inland city in Florida to resort to a seawater system, as difficult as that might be. There would be powerful opposition to building a large de-salting plant at the nearest point on the East Coast, where it might conflict with the NASA [National Aeronautics and Space Administration] launch complex at the Kennedy Space Center [Florida]. An offshore site might work.

Even Atlanta [Georgia], 300 miles from the ocean, may someday have to turn to seawater. Since the 1950s, when no one foresaw the possibility of long-term water shortages for Atlanta, a population explosion accompanied by an extended drought of unprecedented severity has lowered water levels drastically in Lake Lanier and Lake Allatoona—two huge reservoirs serving the area.

Lowering Sea Levels

Clearly, planning and developing large numbers of seawater desalting plants will cause many problems, but the desalting plants that cause local problems may in the aggregate help against a huge global problem—the rise of sea levels due to the melting of ice in mountain ranges and at the poles.

4

Desalination Is Too Expensive to Be a Solution to Fresh Water Shortages

Kris De Decker

Kris De Decker is a journalist and the founder and publisher of Low-tech Magazine, *an Internet journal that addresses the impact of technology on society.*

As fresh water resources deplete, various nations and communities are turning to desalination of seawater as a solution to water shortages. Besides its documented environmental harms, desalination is an energy-intensive process that consumes 6 kilowatt-hours of electricity to make 1 cubic meter of fresh water. In addition, power plants utilize fresh water sources as cooling agents, thus creating a vicious cycle in which fresh water is depleted to make fresh water. Even if desalination plants improve their efficiency, population increases and energy demands will not likely permit the process to become a viable answer to the fresh water crisis.

Desalination—the process of turning seawater into fresh water—is increasingly becoming the world's solution to a growing water shortage problem. But if we count on the oceans to fulfill our future need, we have to find an extra 30.000 terawatt-hours of energy—twice the current global electricity production figure.

We are running out of fresh water. In arid and semi-arid regions, rivers run dry before they reach the sea. In many parts of the world, groundwater tables are falling rapidly due to the over pumping of water. Agriculture, the main culprit, can be accountable for more than 70 percent of total water use worldwide.

Virtual Water: Hidden Water Use in Everyday Life

In rich nations, people use 100 to 200 litres of tap water a day. But this number becomes almost insignificant when compared to the hidden ('virtual') water consumption required to feed (and dress) every one of us. Around 300 litres of water is needed for the production of a mere two eggs, one bag of potato crisps or two cups of coffee.

A cotton t-shirt or a 300g [gram] steak demands a hefty 5.000 litres of water. Installing a water saving showerhead is not going to save us from trouble. World population is growing, and as more people become richer, the consumption of meat and dairy products increases.

According to the International Water Management Institute, by 2050, the withdrawal of water by the global agricultural sector alone will grow by 75 percent. This projected growth would mean that we would have to find another 5.000 cubic kilometres of fresh water to produce the world's meal demand.

Draining Aquifers and Harvesting Seawater

Extracting that supplement from groundwater and rivers is a recipe for disaster. In many arid regions, agriculture is dependent on 'fossil water'—like fossil fuels, this water source is non-renewable. It was captured in underground reservoirs as a result of melting glaciers thousands of years ago. These so-called aquifers are depleting rapidly. Even the renewable groundwater is being pumped up faster than nature can compensate.

In areas with a concentration of human activity (urbanisation, agriculture, industry) groundwater tables fall by 2 to 10 metres a year. At this rate our most important fresh water sources will be used up faster than the remaining fossil fuel reserves. Around 2 billion people are dependent on groundwater for drinking, while more than 1 billion people eat food that is cultivated by it.

According to the World Water Council, a vegetarian diet consumes only half as much water as a typical meat diet. Collecting rainfall would also prove to be a low-tech solution. But unfortunately, harvesting the vast reserves of seawater is a solution that fits our way of thinking better.

Some basic calculations demonstrate that desalination will get us nowhere, since it replaces the water shortage by an energy shortage problem.

Desalination Is Too Energy Intensive

Desalination has become the "solution" of countries facing water shortage problems: Australia, Spain and China, to name a few. Even England has plans to build a water factory on the banks of the river Thames. Some basic calculations, however, demonstrate that desalination will get us nowhere, since it replaces the water shortage by an energy shortage problem.

Most scientific sources report a power consumption of around 6 kilowatt-hours for producing 1 cubic metre of fresh water out of seawater. If we choose to 'create' the 5.000 km^3 of water for agriculture by desalination, we need 30.000 terawatt-hours of energy. That is twice the worldwide electricity production today. Not to mention the exponentially increasing amount of water used by industrial processes (when people get richer, they also buy more cars and computers).

Taking into account that the world is already facing an energy crisis to which no one has an answer, desalination comes to a dead end. Even without a massive effort in desalination technology, the International Energy Association is expecting a doubling of electricity use by 2030.

Over and above this, energy production in itself is also water intensive (that consumption is included in the fast growing amount of industrial fresh water use). For every kilowatt-hour of electricity, an energy plant (fossil or nuclear) consumes 140 to 180 litres of cooling water. Which means that the desalination of 1 cubic metre of water asks 1 cubic metre of water (6x140/180 = 840/1080 litres = 0,84/1,08m³).

In other words, we should use salt water as cooling water. If not, water production will consume all available energy, and energy production will consume all available water.

Desalination is not a sustainable solution.

The amount of cooling water withdrawn by energy plants is not completely lost. Only a small portion evaporates. The remaining water flows back into the rivers or lakes. The problem lies in the obtainability of the water. In the United States for example, energy production already competes with agriculture for available fresh water.

Desalination will get more efficient—around 4 percent a year, according to the industry. But with the projected 3 kilowatt-hour per m³ (by late twenties), we are still on track to doubling electricity consumption.

Ignoring the Problems of Desalination

Desalination is not a sustainable solution. Plants dump salt from the filtered water back into the ocean, and the higher the waters salt content, the more energy it takes to turn it into fresh water. The cycle continues.

Drilling for new fossil groundwater reserves or recycling waste-water—the latter option uses the same technology as desalination—are more energy efficient alternatives. According to the World Wildlife Fund, who in June [2007] introduced a report on the ecological consequences of the technology for marine life, both strategies only need one eighth of the energy used by desalinating seawater.

It would, however, still boil down to the production of an extra 3.750 terawatt-hour of electricity—a doubling of the worldwide nuclear energy capacity.

5

Desalination Threatens the Environment and Public Health

Food & Water Watch

Food & Water Watch is a nonprofit organization based in Washington, D.C. Its mission is to ensure that the fish and water resources of the United States and other nations are sustainable and consumable. The organization also focuses on the importance of keeping these food and water resources within the public commons and not under corporate control.

Desalination of seawater is a costly process, but it is also one that poses potential dangers to the environment and public health. Desalination plants utilize pumps to move the seawater through the desalination system. With vacuum tubes placed in the sea, these pumps suck in and kill off fish and other marine life. The energy required to operate these pumps typically requires the burning of fossil fuels, meaning the process is also a contributor to greenhouse emissions. Beyond these hazards, desalination cannot yet completely rid the collected water of harmful chemicals, such as boron, which may then end up in drinking water; nor can the system process all the water it intakes, leaving a percentage with high concentrations of salts, heavy metals, and other poisons. This unusable water becomes a hazard in itself if it accidentally leaks back into groundwater reserves. In the quest for more fresh water, desalination, therefore, is far from a healthy and environmentally friendly solution.

While numbers do a good job of illustrating the pure financial cost of desalination, they do not do justice to the full expense. Additional costs borne by the public include damage to the environment, danger to the public health and other external considerations.

Not surprisingly, these costs are often glossed over when proposals are made. According to the National Research Council report ["Desalination: A National Perspective," in 2008], external costs are rarely evaluated accurately when desalination projects are proposed and sometimes ignored completely. But these costs can be significant.

Ocean Desalination Contributes to Global Warming

Every step of reverse osmosis,[1] from the water intake to the high-pressure pumps, transport and waste disposal systems, requires large amounts of energy. In addition, the saltier the source water, the more energy required to remove the salt. Seawater is the most concentrated source water solution there is, which means that ocean desalination is the most energy intensive desalination process.

Based on cost estimates from the National Research Council report, seawater desalination in California takes nine times as much energy as surface water treatment and 14 times as much energy as groundwater production. Meanwhile, very few desalination plants use renewable energy sources. Surfrider Foundation and San Diego Coastkeeper estimated that a 53 million gallon-per-day desalination plant would cause nearly double the emissions of treating and reusing the same amount of water. Ironically, these emissions contribute to global climate change, which will only quicken the droughts and water shortages that desalination is supposed to help us avoid.

1. Reverse osmosis is a desalination technique that involves the pumping of seawater or brackish water over pourous, synthetic membranes. The water passes through the membranes while the salt and other solids do not.

Ocean Desalination Damages Marine Life

Ocean desalination plants can wreak havoc on marine life and commercial fisheries. Many proposed coastal plants rely on power plants to pull in ocean water. These power plants use outdated "once-through cooling water intake structures" that cool the plants by pulling in large quantities of seawater. Desalination plants located next to these facilities take a portion of the outgoing water from these systems for their water supply.

The problem here is that these structures suck in a lot more than seawater—they also bring marine life that dies in the machinery. According to EPA [Environmental Protection Agency], these intake structures kill at least 3.4 billion fish and other organisms annually. Larger organisms are trapped against the intake screens, and smaller ones, such as fish eggs and larvae, are drawn through the intake screens and destroyed in the cooling system. As a result, fishermen lose at least 165 million pounds of fish today and 717.1 million pounds of potential future catch. This is equivalent to a $212.5 million economic loss to anglers and commercial fishermen.

According to EPA, [power plant] intake structures kill at least 3.4 billion fish and other organisms annually.

California's power plant intake structures alone are responsible for the destruction of at least 312.9 million organisms each year, resulting in the lost catch of at least 28.9 million pounds of fish and 43.6 million pounds of potential future catch. This amounts to a $13.6 million loss to fishermen.

Ocean Desalination Pollutes

A large amount of the water that exits desalination plants is concentrated waste rather than drinking water. This is because reverse osmosis cannot separate salt from all the water that enters the plant. Depending on the equipment, reverse osmosis desalination membranes can reclaim 60 percent to 85 percent of brackish water and only 35 percent to 60 percent of ocean water. For example, the proposed plant in Carlsbad, California, will desalinate only half of the water that enters the plant.

The significant portion of remaining water contains the salts and other dissolved solids from source water, but at dangerous concentrations two to 10 times higher than the original water. In addition, it contains some or all of the scale inhibitors, acids, coagulants, ferric chloride, flocculents, cationic polymer, chlorines, bisulfites and hydrogen peroxides used to treat the feed water and clean the membranes, along with heavy metals from contact with plant machinery.

The significant portion of remaining water [after the desalination process] contains the salts and other dissolved solids from source water, but at dangerous concentrations two to 10 times higher than the original water.

There is simply nowhere to put this liquid waste that does not pose a danger to our water systems. Most coastal plants dump their waste directly into the ocean, increasing the salinity and temperature and decreasing the water quality in the surrounding ecosystem.

Proponents argue that by dumping the toxic chemicals into a very large body of water, they will spread out and become less dangerous. While this may be true of some substances, such as salt, others, such as heavy metals, remain just as dangerous after dilution.

Further, when concentrated waste is dumped directly into the ocean, it may have localized impacts, such as killing marine organisms or displacing them from their natural habitat. This raises particular problems when the affected marine life communities are rare or of special interest.

The second most common disposal method for desalinated waste is not appropriate for seawater desalination. This method involves transporting the wastes to a nearby sewage treatment plant. However, seawater waste is more concentrated than waste from brackish plants. It can overload the treatment system and prohibit reuse of the wastewater because standard treatments cannot remove contaminants from the seawater waste.

Other less common disposal methods include injecting waste into wells, leaving it in open ponds to evaporate or spraying it on crops—all of which run the risk of having it leak into clean groundwater. Only one method—called Zero Liquid Discharge—does not have a liquid byproduct, but it is so expensive and energy intensive that it is not a realistic option for any existing plant.

Desalted water also puts the drinking water supply at risk because both seawater and brackish water can contain chemicals that freshwater does not.

Ocean Desalination Threatens Coastal Resources

In addition to coastal pollution, desalination can contribute to unwise coastal over-development. One drawback to this is that industrial plants along the coast can impair views and interfere with the recreational use of seawater.

Another is that building water-producing facilities in a region that otherwise wouldn't have sufficient water encourages unsound coastal management. In Huntington Beach, California, for example, a proposed desalination project failed to identify any current users for its water. Indeed, the city's Urban Water Management Plan has not identified ocean desalination as a necessary component of expected growth.

Ocean Desalination Threatens Public Health

Environmental damage is not the only danger from ocean desalination. Desalted water also puts the drinking water supply at risk because both seawater and brackish water can contain chemicals that freshwater does not. These contaminants include chemicals such as endocrine disruptors, pharmaceuticals, personal care products and toxins from marine algae. Some of these contaminants may not be adequately removed in the reverse osmosis process.

Boron is a chemical of particular concern because much higher levels are found in seawater than freshwater. However, membranes can remove only between 50 and 70 percent of this element. The rest is concentrated in the product water, which enters the drinking water system. While it is possible to remove more boron with a second process, existing plants don't because it is too costly.

This is a major problem for the drinking water system because boron is known to cause reproductive and developmental problems in experimental animals and irritation of the human digestive tract. Moreover, the world's largest ocean desalination plant in Ashkelon, Israel found that the boron in the desalted water acted as an herbicide when applied to crops.

Current drinking water regulations do not protect the public from boron. Recently, EPA made the preliminary determination that it would not regulate the element as a primary contaminant under the Safe Drinking Water Act because of its low occurrence in traditional sources of drinking water. However, the studies that EPA used to make this decision did not take into account the hike in boron levels that would occur if desalted water was to be added to the system.

6

Human Ingenuity Will Eventually Solve the Looming Fresh Water Shortage

Brian Fagan

Brian Fagan is an emeritus professor of anthropology at the University of California in Santa Barbara. He is a contributing editor to American Archaeology *and* Discover Archaeology *magazines as well as the author of several books including* Elixir: A History of Water and Humankind.

Humanity has always created innovative methods of fulfilling its need for fresh water. However, with dwindling fresh water stocks and a generally irresponsible attitude toward their use, the modern era must act to ensure everyone has enough water to drink. Current remedies, including everything from desalination of seawater to more efficient residential water use, are part of the answer. The real solution, though, will depend on changing people's mindset about water and forcing them to recognize its value and the need to conserve remaining resources. Thankfully, history demonstrates that humanity has developed various strategies for preserving and supplying fresh water, so there is every reason to expect contemporary society will do so as well. However, such inventiveness will come only if people regain their lost respect for water and recognize that its supply is finite.

This may seem like a surprising statement, but the world's supply of fresh water is finite. As global population rises, the demand for food—and the water that produces it—grows inexorably. Globally, farming accounts for 70 per cent of our withdrawals from this fixed "bank account", this in the face of ever-greater domestic and industrial usage.

Water tables are falling in many parts of the world. Himalayan glaciers will shrink massively in the next century, reducing natural water storage in the mountains. The shortfalls will have to come from groundwater and surface storage. Many great rivers have drastically diminished flows.

Much of the world's water is still unpriced, but it is now the most valuable commodity in the world.

Bangladesh is suffering from the diversion of Ganges River water and increased salinisation. Underground aquifers in many places are shrinking so rapidly that NASA [National Aeronautics and Space Administration] satellites are detecting changes in the Earth's gravity. The Water Resources Group has estimated that India may face a 50 per cent lag in water availability relative to demand by 2030 and that global availability may lag demand by as much as 40 per cent; the statistics have been questioned. Sixty years ago, the world's population was about 1.25 billion people; few people, even in arid lands, worried about water supplies. Then came the Green Revolution, with its new, high-yielding crops, which depend on fertilisers and a great deal more irrigated farming. Global populations skyrocketed to nearly seven billion by 2009, with a projected nine billion by 2050. By the same year, the five hundred million people living in areas chronically short of water in the year 2000 will have grown by 45 per cent to four billion. A billion of us currently go hungry because there is not enough water to grow food. Much of the world's water is still unpriced, but it is now the most valuable commodity in the world. To compound the problem, 60 per cent of the world's people live in crowded river basins shared by several countries, often with daggers drawn.

The Looming Cataclysm

The problems are acute, especially in arid areas with growing populations, where boreholes and aquifers are thought to be the answer. Seemingly a miraculous solution, but not if the drawdown exceeds the replenishment rate, as is the case with the ground water beneath a now-sinking Mexico City's 20 million inhabitants and with Bangkok [Thailand], Buenos Aires [Argentina] and Jakarta [Indonesia], where pollution and rising salt levels combine with overdrafting.

Yes, there will be shortfalls, people will go thirsty and die, but in the end, as has happened so many times in the past, human ingenuity, quite apart from technology, will find solutions.

In China, deep groundwater levels have dropped as much as 295ft (90m) in places. We have perforated the Earth's surface with boreholes to deplete a resource that we all, ultimately, hold in common. Now we stand at the threshold of what I call a third stage in our relationship with water; one where, apparently, cataclysm looms on every side. Vivid Doomsday scenarios espoused by numerous writers have Phoenix [Arizona] imploding as its water supplies fail, the Nile drying up, tens of thousands of people crossing national boundaries to find water.

Futurist after futurist warns that water wars are a certainty in coming centuries. Alas, at least some of these cataclysms could descend upon us if we persist in denying the seriousness of the water crisis and deluding ourselves into thinking that uncontrolled growth and more dams are the solution. They are not.

Yes, there will be shortfalls, people will go thirsty and die, but in the end, as has happened so many times in the past, human ingenuity, quite apart from technology, will find solutions. And in the process, we will develop new, much more respectful relationships with water, even if they do not necessarily have the profound spiritual intertwinings of earlier times.

Short-Term Solutions

In the short term, there are four potential ways of improving the situation, but none of them will solve the problem of chronic overdrawing. One lies in spending large sums on systematic improvements to storage and delivery, to the infrastructure behind water supplies. Underground reservoirs have potential. So do simple things like replacing leaking pipes, lining earth-bottomed canals and irrigating plants at their roots with just the right amount of water, among many others. A second solution also makes sense: make farming less thirsty, by using drought-resistant, higher-yielding, even genetically-modified crops. This is much easier said than done, for significant technological breakthroughs lie a long way in the future. Also, we should not forget that planting more crops means more use of water, since each plant transpires vapour into the atmosphere through photosynthesis. One possible solution may lie in developing plants that can grow using saline water but, again, this development is in the future. Then there's another seemingly attractive option: desalinisation. Surprisingly, this has been around a long time. Aristotle remarked that "salt water, when it turns to steam, becomes sweet and the steam does not form salt water when it condenses". Julius Caesar's legions drank fresh water condensed from sea water during his siege of Alexandria in 48–47 BCE. As self-appointed visionaries keep reminding us, desalinisation seems like the answer to all our problems but, in spite of improvements in efficiency, there remain significant environmental and technical problems. Desalinisation, which involves creating and recondensing steam, consumes prodigious amounts of energy, even in its most efficient iterations, so it is currently confined to nations where oil is cheap and abundant.

Nearly half the existing desalinisation plants are in the Arabian Peninsula and along the Persian Gulf, especially in Saudi Arabia and the Gulf states. In most other places, the cost of desalinisation is three or four times that of conventional water sources.

The cost of oil is rising, so the alternatives are either coal or nuclear power, both of which have their own environmental consequences and political baggage. Desalinisation plants operate along sea coasts; many of the most water-hungry areas are far inland, thereby adding huge transport costs to the already high price of a gallon of desalinised water. What, also, are we to do with the brine resulting from desalinisation, which has to be disposed of? Once again, breakthroughs lie in the long-term future. At present, desalinisation is no panacea, for it contributes only about 0.4 per cent of global water supplies.

Even in dry parts of the world where every drop is precious, the price of water seldom reflects its true scarcity.

Water Conservation and a New Water Market

Finally, there's conservation, which involves both profound changes in our mindsets and completely new attitudes toward water as a marketable commodity. Water is scarce, but it is also a complicated thing to market. It is difficult to move, hard to measure accurately in large quantities and complex to price and charge for. Most people resent paying for water, for they think it should be free or very cheap. Even in dry parts of the world where every drop is precious, the price of water seldom reflects its true scarcity. However, we are entering an era of potentially ferocious trading in water rights and a time when water could cost more than oil, as managing demand becomes an international priority. It's no coincidence that privately owned companies are quietly and aggressively purchasing water rights in many countries. Increasingly, municipal and other authorities are pricing water according to usage. Judging from experience in Australia, Los Angeles [California] and other water markets, the strategy leads to reduced water use, especially when combined with measures to save water, such as reduced-flow toilets and strict timetables for watering. Like oil, water is a commodity that will be the subject of market forces, with price mechanisms that will bring supply and demand into balance. Once water is priced properly, the economics of international trade may encourage water-rich countries to produce water-intensive goods and arid ones to make those that are water-light. Mindsets are notoriously difficult to change, especially in societies accustomed to abundance and seemingly unlimited water supplies.

Humans have managed water successfully for thousands of years in ways that are often far from the historical radar screen.

Using the forces of the marketplace and stricter allocations will not be strategies of first choice, especially in urban settings with high levels of poverty. Nor will conservation in the form of another commonly proposed measure, yet more dam construction, prove effective. History from the near and remote past tells us that dams are no panacea, for they silt up and silt has to be removed or the dam becomes shallower and ever less useful. And, even more important, where is the water to fill them going to come from? No dam ever creates water; it merely captures what is a finite supply. How can new dams provide more water in the era of prolonged global drought that lies ahead? Besides, there's adequate dam capacity in the

51

American West to store any water that will come from the smaller snowpacks of future decades. Short of creating more water, more efficient allocation, extensive water recycling for landscaping and other purposes, drastic reductions in agribusiness water subsidies and miserly use of current supplies are some viable strategies for the future. And this kind of conservation, on scales small and large, is the responsibility of us all. Our survival depends upon it. We have much to learn about water conservation from the experience of our ancestors. Humans have managed water successfully for thousands of years in ways that are often far from the historical radar screen. We learn from their experiences that it is the simple and ingenious that often works best—local water schemes, decisions about sharing and management made by kin, family and small communities. These experiences also teach us that self-sustainability is attainable.

Forcing Humanity to Think Differently About Water

Such ingenuity comes in many forms. It may be a simple idea in the field or, in this day and age, more likely the inspiration for a social and political initiative that changes the way people think. We are moving into an entirely new water future, where equity of use, sustainability to protect future generations and affordability for everyone are major components.

A new paradigm for water management, based on well-defined priorities in which all stakeholders have a voice, will have to govern our future water use. Our salvation lies in long-term thinking, in decisive political leadership and in a reordering of financial priorities for, after all, investing heavily in water management will alleviate much disease and poverty automatically. Above all, the future will need a shift in our relationship with water to one that equates, at least approximately, with that of those who went before us—characterised by a studied caring and reverence.

7

Fresh Water Is Becoming a Privatized Commodity Instead of a Public Trust

Jeneen Interlandi with Ryan Tracy

Jeneen Interlandi is a science and health reporter for Newsweek. *Ryan Tracy was a reporter at* Newsweek *but now is a writer for Dow Jones Newswires.*

As a fresh water crisis looms, many private companies are buying up water rights in various nations. These corporations are then selling the water to local consumers or shipping it to other parts of the globe that may have little or no access to fresh water. A water market is therefore arising in which this vital resource is treated as a commodity to be bought and sold. While some people protest the notion that water is a commodity, municipalities in water-rich areas of countries like the United States and Canada are motivated to accept the new paradigm because it can bring jobs in bottling plants or even take the cost burden off public utilities that struggle to update and repair decaying water networks. Some advocates even argue that turning water into a commodity is a necessary means of convincing the public to treat water use and conservation more seriously.

Sitka, Alaska, is home to one of the world's most spectacular lakes. Nestled into a U-shaped valley of dense forests and majestic peaks, and fed by snowpack and glaciers, the reservoir, named Blue Lake for its deep blue hues, holds trillions of gallons of water so pure it requires no treatment. The city's tiny population—fewer than 10,000 people spread across 5,000 square miles—makes this an embarrassment of riches. Every year, as countries around the world struggle to meet the water needs of their citizens, 6.2 billion gallons of Sitka's reserves go unused. That could soon change. In a few months, if all goes according to plan, 80 million gallons of Blue Lake water will be siphoned into the kind of tankers normally reserved for oil—and shipped to a bulk bottling facility near Mumbai [India]. From there it will be dispersed among several drought-plagued cities throughout the Middle East. The project is the brainchild of two American companies. One, True Alaska Bottling, has purchased the rights to transfer 3 billion gallons of water a year from Sitka's bountiful reserves. The other, S2C Global, is building the water-processing facility in India. If the companies succeed, they will have brought what Sitka hopes will be a $90 million industry to their city, not to mention a solution to one of the world's most pressing climate conundrums. They will also have turned life's most essential molecule into a global commodity.

Treating Water as a Commodity

The transfer of water is nothing new. New York City is supplied by a web of tunnels and pipes that stretch 125 miles north into the Catskills Mountains; Southern California gets its water from the Sierra Nevada Mountains and the Colorado River Basin, which are hundreds of miles to the north and west, respectively. The distance between Alaska and India is much farther, to be sure. But it's not the distance that worries critics. It's the transfer of so much water from public hands to private ones. "Water has been a public resource under public domain for more than 2,000 years," says James Olson, an attorney who specializes in water rights. "Ceding it to private entities feels both morally wrong and dangerous."

Everyone agrees that we are in the midst of a global fresh-water crisis. Around the world, rivers, lakes, and aquifers are dwindling faster than Mother Nature can possibly replenish them; industrial and household chemicals are rapidly polluting what's left. Meanwhile, global population is ticking skyward. Goldman Sachs estimates that global water consumption is doubling every 20 years, and the United Nations expects demand to outstrip supply by more than 30 percent come 2040.

Proponents of privatization say . . . only the invisible hand can bring supply and demand into harmony, and only market pricing will drive water use down enough to make a dent in water scarcity.

Proponents of privatization say markets are the best way to solve that problem: only the invisible hand can bring supply and demand into harmony, and only market pricing will drive water use down enough to make a dent in water scarcity. But the benefits of the market come at a price. By definition, a commodity is sold to the highest bidder, not the customer with the most compelling moral claim. As the crisis worsens, companies like True Alaska that own the rights to vast stores of water (and have the capacity to move it in bulk) won't necessarily weigh the needs of wealthy water-guzzling companies like Coca-Cola or Nestlé against those of water-starved communities in Phoenix [Arizona] or Ghana [in western Africa]; privately owned water utilities will charge what the market can bear, and spend as little as they can get away with on maintenance and environmental protection. Other commodities are subject to the same laws, of course. But with energy, or food, customers have options: they can switch from oil to natural gas, or eat more chicken and less beef. There is no substitute for water, not even Coca-Cola. And, of course, those other things don't just fall from the sky on whoever happens to be lucky enough to be living below. "Markets don't care about the environment," says Olson. "And they don't care about human rights. They care about profit."

Global Divisions

In the developed world—America especially—it's easy to take water for granted. Turn on any tap, and it comes rushing out, clean and plentiful, even in the arid Southwest, where the Colorado River Basin is struggling through its 11th year of drought; in most cities a month's supply still costs less than premium cable or a generous cell-phone plan. Many of us have no idea where our water comes from, let alone who owns it. In fact, most of us would probably agree that water is too precious for anybody to own. But the rights to divert water—from a river or lake or underground aquifer—are indeed sellable commodities; so too are the plants and pipes that process that water and deliver it to our taps. And as demand outstrips supply, those commodities are set to appreciate precipitously. According to a 2009 report by the World Bank, private investment in the water industry is set to double in the next five years; the water-supply market alone will increase by 20 percent.

[Critics fear that] eventually . . . every last drop will be privately controlled. And when that happens, the world will find itself divided along a new set of boundaries: water haves on one side, water have-nots on the other.

Unlike the villain in James Bond's *Quantum of Solace* who hatched a secret plot to monopolize Bolivia's fresh-water supply, the real water barons cannot be reduced to a simple archetype. They include a diverse array of buyers and sellers—from multinational water giants like Suez and Veolia that together deliver water to some 260 million taps around the world, to wildcatter oil converts like T. Boone Pickens who wants to sell the water under his Texas Panhandle ranch to thirsty cities like Dallas. "The water market has become much more sophisticated in the last two decades," says Clay Landry, director of WestWater Research, a consulting firm that specializes in water rights. "It's gone from parochial transactions—back-of-the-truck, handshake-type deals—to a serious market with increasingly serious players."

Eventually, Olson worries, every last drop will be privately controlled. And when that happens, the world will find itself divided along a new set of boundaries: water haves on one side, water have-nots on the other. The winners (Canada, Alaska, Russia) and losers (India, Syria, Jordan) will be different from those of the oil conflicts of the 20th century, but the bottom line will be much the same: countries that have the means to exploit large reserves will prosper. The rest will be left to fight over ever-shrinking reserves. Some will go to war.

Privatizing to Save Costs of Infrastructure Repairs and Updates

Until recently, water privatization was an almost exclusively Third World issue. In the late 1990s the World Bank infamously required scores of impoverished countries—most notably Bolivia—to privatize their water supplies as a condition of desperately needed economic assistance. The hope was that markets would eliminate corruption and big multinationals would invest the resources needed to bring more water to more people. By 2000, Bolivian citizens had taken to the streets in a string of violent protests. Bechtel—the multinational corporation that had leased their pipes and plants—had more than doubled water rates, leaving tens of thousands of Bolivians who couldn't pay without any water whatsoever. The company said price hikes were needed to repair and expand the dilapidated infrastructure. Critics insisted they served only to maintain unrealistic profit margins. Either way, the rioters sent the companies packing; by 2001, the public utility had resumed control.

These days, global water barons have set their sights on a more appealing target: countries with dwindling water supplies and aging infrastructure, but better economies than Bolivia's. "These are the countries that can afford to pay," says Olson. "They've got huge infrastructure needs, shrinking water reserves, and money."

Nowhere is this truer than China. As the water table under Beijing plummets, wells dug around the city must reach ever-greater depths (nearly two thirds of a mile or more, according to a recent World Bank report) to hit fresh water. That has made water drilling more costly and water contracts more lucrative. Since 2000, when the country opened its municipal services to foreign investment, the number of private water utilities has skyrocketed. But as private companies absorb water systems throughout the country, the cost of water has risen precipitously. "It's more than most families can afford to pay," says Ge Yun, an economist with the Xinjiang Conservation Fund. "So as more water goes private, fewer people have access to it."

Elected officials can use the profits from water sales to balance city budgets, while simultaneously offloading the huge cost of repairing and expanding infrastructure . . . to companies that promise both jobs and economy-stimulating profits.

In the U.S., federal funds for repairing water infrastructure—most of which was built around the same time that Henry Ford built the first Model T—are sorely lacking. The [Barack] Obama administration has secured just $6 billion for repairs that the EPA [Environmental Protection Agency] estimates will cost $300 billion. Meanwhile, more than half a million pipes burst every year, according to the American Water Works Association, and more than 6 billion gallons of water are lost to leaky pipes. In response to the funding gap, hundreds of U.S. cities—including Pittsburgh [Pennsylvania], Chicago [Illinois], and Santa Fe, N.M.—are now looking to privatize. On its face, the move makes obvious sense: elected officials can use the profits from water sales to balance city budgets, while simultaneously offloading the huge cost of repairing and expanding infrastructure—not to mention the politically unpopular necessity of raising water rates to do so—to companies that promise both jobs and economy-stimulating profits.

Of course, the reality doesn't always meet that ideal. "Because water infrastructure is too expensive to allow multiple providers, the only real competition occurs during the bidding process," says Wenonah Hauter, executive director of the nonprofit, antiprivatization group Food and Water Watch. "After that, the private utility has a virtual monopoly. And because 70 to 80 percent of water and sewer assets are underground, municipalities can have a tough time monitoring a contractor's performance." According to some reports, private operators often reduce the workforce, neglect water conservation, and shift the cost of environmental violations onto the city. For example, when two Veolia-operated plants spilled millions of gallons of sewage into San Francisco Bay, at least one city was forced to make multimillion-dollar upgrades to the offending sewage plant. (Veolia has defended its record.)

Private Water Companies Face Litigation

Even as many U.S. cities look toward ceding their water infrastructure to private interests, others are waging expensive legal battles to get out of such contracts. In 2009 Camden, N.J., sued United Water (an American subsidiary of the French giant Suez) for $29 million in unapproved payments, high unaccounted-for water losses, poor maintenance, and service disruptions. In Milwaukee [Wisconsin] a state audit found that the same company violated its contract by shutting down sewage pumps to save money; the move resulted in billions of gallons of raw sewage spilling into Lake Michigan. And in Gary, Ind., which canceled its contract with United Water after 12 years, critics say privatization more than doubled annual operating costs. "It ends up being a roundabout way to tax people," Hauter says. "Only it's worse than a tax because they don't spend the money maintaining the system."

Representatives of United Water point out that 95 percent of its contracts are in fact renewed and say that a few bad examples don't tell the whole story. "We are dealing with facilities that were designed and built at the end of World War II," says United Water CEO Bertrand Camus. "We have plenty of horror stories on our side, too." The Gary facility, to take one example, went private only after the EPA forced the public utility to find a more experienced operator to solve a range of problems. "Individual municipalities don't have the expertise to employ all the new technology to meet the new standards," Camus says. "We do."

The bottom line is this: that water is essential to life makes it no less expensive to obtain, purify, and deliver, and does nothing to change the fact that as supplies dwindle and demand grows, that expense will only increase.

The bottom line is this: that water is essential to life makes it no less expensive to obtain, purify, and deliver, and does nothing to change the fact that as supplies dwindle and demand grows, that expense will only increase. The World Bank has argued that higher prices are a good thing. Right now, no public utility anywhere prices water based on how scarce it is or how much it costs to deliver, and that, privatization proponents argue, is the root cause of such rampant overuse. If water costs more, they say, we will conserve it better.

Consumers and Suppliers Have No Incentive to Conserve Water

The main problem with this argument is what economists call price inelasticity: no matter what water costs, we still need it to survive. So beyond trimming nonessential uses like lawn maintenance, car washing, and swimming pools, consumers really can't reduce water consumption in proportion to rate increases. "Free-market theory works great for discretionary consumer purchases," says Hauter. "But water is not like other commodities—it's not something people can substitute or choose to forgo." Dozens of studies have found that even with steep rate hikes, consumers tend to reduce water consumption by only a little, and that even in the worst cases, the crunch is disproportionately shouldered by the poor. In the string of droughts that plagued California during the 1980s, for example, doubling the price of water drove household consumption down by a third, but households earning less than $20,000 cut their consumption by half, while households earning more than $100,000 reduced use by only 10 percent.

The biggest winners of a sophisticated water market are likely to be the very few water-rich regions of the global north that can profitably move massive quantities across huge distances.

In fact, critics say, private water companies usually have very little incentive to encourage conservation; after all, when water use falls, revenue declines. In 2005 a second Bolivian riot erupted when another private water company raised rates beyond what average people could afford. The company had dutifully expanded the city's water system to several poor neighborhoods outside the city. But the villagers there, accustomed to life without taps, were obsessive water conservers and hadn't used enough water to make the investment profitable.

The biggest winners of a sophisticated water market are likely to be the very few water-rich regions of the global north that can profitably move massive quantities across huge distances. Russian entrepreneurs want to sell Siberian water to China; Canadian and American ones are vying to sell Canadian water to the Southwestern U.S. So far, such bulk transfers have been impeded by the high cost of tanker ships. Now, thanks to the global recession, the tankers' rates have dropped significantly. If the Sitka plan succeeds, other water-rich cities may soon follow.

Conflict or Cooperation

But in between the countries that will profit from the freshwater crisis, and those that will buy their way out of it, are the countries that have neither water to sell nor money with which to buy it. In fact, if there's one thing water has in common with oil, it's that people will go to war over it. Already, Pakistan has accused India of diverting too much water from rivers running off the Himalayas; India, in turn, is complaining that China's colossal diversion of rivers and aquifers near the countries' shared border will deprive it of its fair share; and Jordan and Syria are bickering over access to flows from a dam the two countries built together.

So what do we do? On the one hand, most of the world views water as a basic human right (the U.N. [United Nations] General Assembly voted unanimously to affirm it as such this July [2010]). On the other, it's becoming so expensive to obtain and supply that most governments cannot afford to shoulder the cost alone. By themselves, markets will never be able to balance these competing realities. That means state and federal governments will have to play a stronger role in managing freshwater resources. In the U.S., investing as much money in water infrastructure as the federal government has invested in other public-works projects would not only create jobs but also alleviate some of the financial pressure that has sent so many municipal governments running to private industry. That is not to say that industry doesn't also have a role to play. With the right incentives, it can develop and supply the technology needed to make water delivery more cost-effective and environmentally sound. Ultimately both public and private entities will have to work together. And soon. Unless we manage our water better now, we will run out. When that happens, no pricing or management scheme in the world will save us.

8

Fresh Water Should Be Treated as a Commodity

Peter Brabeck-Letmathe

Austrian entrepreneur Peter Brabeck-Letmathe is the current chairman and former chief executive officer of Nestlé Group, the largest food corporation in the world. Nestlé's holdings include a bottled water company.

Dwindling fresh water supplies and irresponsible water waste suggest that governments should adopt measures to treat water as a commodity. Because it is so valuable to human existence, it should be priced accordingly. Households should receive subsidized water allowances, but any use beyond that should cost consumers. Industry and agriculture should also bear the expense of their excessive use and waste of water supplies, hopefully pushing these sectors to conserve and recover more fresh water. Conceiving of water as a commodity is an important step in getting everyone to recognize the value of preserving this vital resource.

Arguably, no country understands the water crisis better than South Africa. The Rainbow Nation has had to confront head-on an issue that others are only now beginning to wake up to.

It's fair to say that there aren't many countries that include a reference to the right to access water in their constitutions. Our planet's attitude towards water is wholly unsustainable.

Global water requirements are expected to grow by over 50% over the next 20 years, according to a recent report by McKinsey for the 2030 Water Resources Group, of which Nestlé is a member. By 2030, water withdrawals will exceed natural renewal by more than 60%, mostly at the expense of the water urgently required for the environment. While our collective attention has been focused on depleting supplies of fossil fuels, we have been largely ignoring the simple fact that, unless radical changes are made, we will run out of water first, and soon.

Price Should Reflect Value

The era of water at throwaway prices is coming to an end. I have long argued that we need to set a price that more accurately values our most precious commodity; the OECD [Organization for Economic Co-operation and Development] and the World Bank are also moving in this direction, and have recently published reports suggesting the setting of a better price for water.

While it is a basic human right to have access to subsidised water for hydration and hygiene, why should washing your car, filling a swimming pool or watering a garden be priced in the same way?

Unfortunately, progress has been hampered by a debate that has been polarised and simplistic. Yet the experience of South Africa teaches us that this does not need to be a binary decision. Its introduction of a household monthly allocation via its free basic water subsidy programme allows for basic sanitation, cooking and drinking water, while charging the full cost of the infrastructure for additional use.

Other countries can learn from this step-pricing approach, which recognises that not all water use should be regarded as equal. While it is a basic human right to have access to subsidised water for hydration and hygiene, why should washing your car, filling a swimming pool or watering a garden be priced in the same way? Full cost recovery for these activities will not only ensure that we are more judicious in our use, but will also, crucially, help repair our leaking infrastructure. In the poorest areas, it will also help to extend pipes so that water reaches more homes.

Improving Agricultural Water Use

But any improvements in domestic use will come to nothing if we do not radically alter our approach to agriculture, which takes up about 70% of global water usage. It is here that the greatest difference can be made, but progress has been frustratingly slow to date.

Improving agricultural productivity is absolutely fundamental to helping to address water shortages and increasing the "crop per drop", particularly in the developing world.

Measures such as no-tillage farming, improved drainage, drip and sprinkler irrigation and crop yield enhancement can all increase output, many of them at relatively low cost.

A rise in water prices would also improve efficiency in this area. A recent [March 2010] OECD report into water management in agriculture, for example, has shown that, in areas where the price of water for agriculture has increased, agricultural production has been unaffected. It highlights the example of Australia, which was able to cut irrigation water use by half without a loss of output.

Even more interesting is the story of the *aflaj*, ancient irrigation systems in Oman, with tradable water rights and more than 4,000 years of efficient and sustainable water use. Water should have an adequate price for any use as a commercial good but, as outlined, different principles apply for water as a social and environmental good.

A Concern for Everyone

It is the responsibility of all involved in working with farmers to help them find ways to improve their water efficiency. For Nestlé, this takes the form of training and the promotion of water stewardship, technical help or even assistance through microfinance. This is as important to us as our commitment to reducing water waste in our own business. After all, industry uses twice as much water as households, and often in a more inefficient way.

Governments too have to recognise water for the precious commodity that it is, and price it accordingly. If the current focus on South Africa [host of the 2010 World Cup] can help highlight the benefits of flexible pricing, this will have been a successful World Cup.

9

Fresh Water Should Be Treated as a Human Right

Maude Barlow

Canadian author and activist Maude Barlow is the co-founder of the Blue Planet Project, an international organization devoted to preserving the right to water for all people. She also served as the senior advisor on water to the sixty-third president of the United Nations General Assembly.

The governments of the United States and Canada are colluding with corporations to privatize water rights and secure vast re-serves as strategic resources for governmental, industrial, and military use. Only these two countries have consistently impeded international attempts to codify water as a human right that should be shared by all. Citizens need to put pressure on these governments to endorse a proposed United Nation's covenant to recognize water as public resource that should be conserved, not commoditized.

It's a colossal failure of political foresight that water has not emerged as an important issue in the U.S. Presidential campaign [of 2008]. The links between oil, war, and U.S. foreign policy are well known. But water—whether we treat it as a public good or as a commodity that can be bought and sold—will in large part determine whether our future is peaceful or perilous.

Americans use water even more wastefully than oil. The U.S relies on non-renewable groundwater for 50 percent of its daily use, and 36 states now face serious water shortages, some verging on crisis.

Meanwhile, dwindling freshwater supplies around the world, inequitable access to water, and corporate control of water, together with impending climate change from fossil fuel emissions, have created a life-or-death situation across the planet.

Water has become a key strategic security and foreign policy priority for the United States government.

Both Democrats and Republicans have emphasized loosening U.S. dependence on nonrenewable energy resources in their platforms, but neither party gives significant air time to the threats posed by water shortages.

This is not to say that no one is paying attention. In fact, water has become a key strategic security and foreign policy priority for the United States government.

The United States and Canada Bid to Secure Water Resources

Corporate interests have pursued schemes to privatize, commodify, and export water for decades. We have seen how this plays out in Canada. For instance, in the late 1990s, Sun Belt Water, Inc., sued the Canadian government under NAFTA [North American Free Trade Agreement] because British Columbia [B.C.] banned water exports, preventing a deal that would have sent B.C. water to California. Corporations have also made attempts to ship Canadian water as far as Asia and the Middle East, proposals that fizzled after fierce opposition from public citizens who were beginning to understand the dangers of permanently removing water from local ecosystems and placing it under corporate control.

Now the Pentagon, as well as various U.S. security think tanks, have decided that water supplies, like energy supplies, must be secured if the United States is to maintain its current economic and military power in the world. And the United States is exerting pressure to access Canadian water, despite Canada's own shortages.

Under the name, "North American Future 2025 Project," the U.S. Center for Strategic and International Studies (CSIS) brought together high level government officials and business executives from Canada, the United States, and Mexico for a series of six meetings to discuss a wide range of issues related to the Security and Prosperity Partnership, a controversial and tightly guarded set of negotiations to expand NAFTA.

"As ... globalization continues and the balance of power potentially shifts, and risks to global security evolve, it is only prudent for Canadian, Mexican, and U.S. policymakers to contemplate a North American security architecture that could effectively deal with security threats that can be foreseen in 2025," said a leaked copy of a CSIS backgrounder.

On the agenda for one of two meetings in Calgary were, "water consumption, water transfers, and artificial diversions of bulk water" with the aim of achieving "joint optimum utilization of the available water."

The Importance of Water in Developing Oil Resources

The water and security connection deepens with the fact that Sandia National Laboratories, a vital partner with CSIS in its Global Water Futures Project, also plays a major role in military security in the United States. While Sandia is technically owned by the U.S. government, and reports to the Department of Energy's National Nuclear Security Administration, its management is contracted out to Lockheed Martin, the world's biggest weapons manufacturer.

Ralph Pentland, water consultant and primary author of the Canadian government's Federal Water Policy in 1987, believes that the purpose of these cross-border discussions is to secure sufficient water for Alberta tar sands production in order to ensure uninterrupted oil supplies to the United States. Energy extraction would be far more attractive if a new source of water—potentially from northern Canada—could be brought to the tar sands through pipelines or other diversions. As long as the water doesn't cross the international border, it is within Alberta's power to do this.

Schemes to displace water from one ecosystem to another in the service of corporate profit are an environmental problem for the entire planet.

These schemes to displace water from one ecosystem to another in the service of corporate profit are an environmental problem for the entire planet, which is another reason why water must form a crucial part of any progressive discussion around U.S. dependence on foreign energy resources.

Corporate interests understand the connection and are using it to make their case for private solutions to the water crisis. In language that will be familiar to critics who argued that the United States invaded Iraq not for democracy but for access to oil and profits for corporations, a 2005 report from CSIS's Global Water Futures project had this to say about water:

> Water issues are critical to U.S. national security and integral to upholding American values of humanitarianism and democratic development. Moreover, engagement with international water issues guarantees business opportunity for the U.S. private sector, which is well positioned to contribute to development and reap economic reward.

Many Nations Accept Water as a Human Right

Clearly, the powers that be in the United States have decided that water is not a public good but a private resource that must be secured by whatever means.

But there are alternatives.

North Americans must learn to live within our means, by conserving water in agriculture and in the home. We could learn from the many examples here and beyond our borders—from the New Mexican "Acequia" system that uses an ancient natural ditch irrigation tradition to distribute water in arid lands to the International Rainwater Harvesting Alliance in Geneva [Switzerland], that works globally to promote sustainable rainwater harvesting programs.

Conservation strategies would undermine the massive investment now going into corporate technological and infrastructure solutions, such as desalination, wastewater reuse, and water transfer projects. And conservation would be many times cheaper, a boon to the public but not to the corporate interests that are currently driving international water agreements.

The U.S. and Canada are the only two countries actively blocking international attempts to recognize water as a human right.

At the grassroots, a global water justice movement is demanding a change in international law to settle once and for all the question of who controls water, and whether responses to the water crisis will ensure water for the public or profits for corporations. Ricardo Petrella has led a movement in Italy to recognize access to water as a basic human right, which has support among politicians at every level. The Coalition in Defense of Public Water in Ecuador is demanding that the government amend the constitution to recognize the right to water. The Coalition Against Water Privatization in South Africa is challenging the practice of water metering before the Johannesburg High Court on the basis that it violates the human rights of Soweto's citizens. Dozens of groups in Mexico have joined COMDA, the Coalition of Mexican Organizations for the Right to Water, a national campaign for a constitutional guarantee of water for the public.

The U.S. and Canada are the only two countries actively blocking international attempts to recognize water as a human right. But movements in both countries are working to change that. A large network of human rights, faith-based, labor, and environmental groups in Canada has formed Canadian Friends of the Right to Water to get the Canadian government to support a U.N. [United Nations] right-to-water covenant. And a network in the United States led by [nonprofit organization] Food and Water Watch is calling for a national water trust to ensure safekeeping of the nation's water assets and a change of government policy on the right to water.

Such campaigns may have a fight ahead of them, but the vision is within reach: a United Nations covenant that recognizes the right of the Earth and other species to clean water, pledges to protect and conserve the world's water supplies, and forms an agreement between those countries who have water and those who don't to work toward local—not corporate—control of water. We must acknowledge water as a fundamental human right for all.

10

Access to Fresh Water May Spark Conflict in the Middle East

Daniel Darling

Daniel Darling is an international military markets analyst with Forecast International Inc., an aerospace and defense research company. He has contributed commentary to the DefenseNews website and his work has been cited in several other military and political journals.

While oil often is perceived as the resource that will eventually generate conflict in the Middle East, water may be a more likely candidate. Middle Eastern nations are largely arid, and their supply of fresh water is limited. History has already proven that these countries have fought for access to water sources, and as their defense budgets and populations grow, there is reason to believe that water scarcity may lead to aggression. In addition, there is the threat that any armed conflict in the region might spur combatants to consider rivers and pipelines as strategic targets, bringing dire repercussions not only to those warring nations but to any other party that relies on that resource.

Mention the words "Middle East" and "war" in the same sentence and almost immediately thoughts turn to religion or oil as the source of conflict. Yet it is a resource more vital than oil that might well determine the outbreak of future wars in the region. While control of oil resources remains a key determinant of outside pressure from non-regional actors, inside the Middle East nations face the very real prospect of a dwindling supply of water.

In this volatile arena burgeoning populations are outstripping supply, in the process creating a looming freshwater crisis. Such a crisis may herald the very resource wars prophesied by environmental scholars, think tanks and government agencies. In such a fragile region the upheaval caused by water disputes in one area could threaten to spill across borders, dragging multiple nations into conflict.

> *Countries such as Jordan and Syria are running out of clean water, while Egypt has become more and more protective of its supply of Nile River waters.*

With water a necessary and finite resource, industrialized nations such as Israel are pressed to improve their water-use technology while insuring hydrological capabilities and supply are not infringed upon by rivals. In other words, water security—both in terms of infrastructure and sources—is an imperative for the tiny state as its consumption rises due to improved living standards and a growing population.

Meanwhile the conflicting pressure caused by declining supply and increasing demand in the Arab world is aggravated by poor management and inefficient usage at the national level. Countries such as Jordan and Syria are running out of clean water, while Egypt has become more and more protective of its supply of Nile River waters.

Flashpoints for Potential Water Conflict

Wars over water resources are not altogether a new concept in the Middle East. The Six-Day War of 1967 was in part an Israeli response to a Syrian attempt to dam the Yarmuk River, which feeds the Jordan River—itself a crucial water source for Israel. Altogether some 30 military clashes over water have occurred since the Israeli state was founded. These have alternately involved Syrian, Jordanian and Lebanese attempts to divert waters flowing from the Banyas, Dan, Hasbani and Yarmuk rivers into Israel. Feuds between Jewish settlers and Palestinians over a well in the West Bank city of Nablus back in March [2010] resulted in the shooting death of a Palestinian by Israeli forces.

While the Levant makes up the obvious flash-point for an outbreak of water-related conflict, to the south it is Yemen that represents the greatest resource-deprived danger in the region.

While the Levant [the geographic region that includes most of modern Lebanon, Syria, Jordan, Israel, the Palestinian territories, and other areas] makes up the obvious flash-point for an outbreak of water-related conflict, to the south it is Yemen that represents the greatest resource-deprived danger in the region. The country is already home to myriad civil pressures involving secessionist violence in the south, an active insurgency along its northern border with Saudi Arabia and an embedded [terrorist group] Al Qaeda presence offering itself up as an alternative to the regime of Yemeni President Ali Abdullah Saleh.

But aggravating the situation are the country's demographic and resource realities. Economically, Yemen remains heavily dependent upon its declining oil production sector. While the country's oil and gas reserves dwindle its population grows at an explosive rate: from 7 million in 1975, to 23 million in 2010—with that figure expected to double by 2035. Mixed in with population pressures, economic problems and civil strife is Yemen's declining freshwater supply which currently provides Yemenis with less than two percent per person of the global average. Cultivation of the mild narcotic, Qat, has only worsened the situation by forcing farmers to drill deeper into underground aquifers rapidly running dry.

The Houthi insurgency to the north has already dragged Saudi Arabia into Yemen's internal conflicts and the prospect of a greater breakdown might persuade other regional and outside actors to involve themselves in Yemeni affairs.

Targeting Water Resources in Military Conflict

Other areas of the region may also see water-related tensions escalate in coming years. Turkey's control of the headwaters of the Tigris and Euphrates rivers places Syria and Iraq at the mercy of Ankara [capital of Turkey] to keep the water flowing. The power thus placed in Turkish hands may serve to undermine relations between a fledgling central Iraqi government and an increasingly confident Turkey determined to play a more active role in the Middle East.

Should the Iranian nuclear issue deteriorate to the point a U.S. and/or Israeli preemptive strike occurs, the infrastructure of the Gulf Arab states—not just in terms of oil, but water—might be impacted. Tehran [capital of Iran] has threatened to retaliate against any first U.S./Israeli strike by launching missile attacks against the Gulf Arab nations allied with Washington [D.C.]. Such aerial assaults might target oil terminals, ports, urban centers and desalinization plants that provide countries like the UAE [United Arab Emirates] with the bulk of its drinking and clean water supply.

Little wonder that the UAE has focused a significant portion of its defense investment over the past several years on building a modern, diverse missile- and air-defense network. This includes the Patriot Advanced Capability (PAC-3) missile defense system, the Russian-built Pantsir-SIE surface-to-air missile and anti-aircraft weapon system, and, most likely, the Theater High Altitude Air Defense (THAAD) system which comes with a base price tag of a cool $1.9 billion.

When the threat to the region from resource pressures is juxtaposed with the ongoing arms spree seen in many of its countries what emerges is a tinderbox. Defense expenditures for the Middle East rose by nearly 31 percent between 2006 and 2010. This upward trend in defense spending is unlikely to stop any time soon—much like the increased demand for water amidst an expanding regional population.

Of course such population and water supply pressures are not unique to the Middle East. Indeed, in 1900 the world population was 1.5 billion; today it is roughly 6.8 billion. Yet while the world's population has grown its water supply has remained static since the dawn of humankind. Water scarcity, therefore, is a very real threat facing the world and one in which the Middle East might merely serve as the first area of conflict in a broader global resource clash.

11

Access to Fresh Water Is a Contentious Issue in the Israel-Palestine Conflict

Wilson Dizard

Wilson Dizard is an undergraduate researcher at Ohio State University and an editorial assistant at the New York Post. *He is currently working on a thesis concerning the impact of climate change on water politics between Palestinians and Israelis.*

Water consumption is unequally divided among Israelis and Palestinians in the Levant. Israel controls most of the water and routinely deny Palestinian pleas for greater access. While the 1995 Oslo II Accords established specific allocations of water for Palestinians in the West Bank and Gaza Strip, these specifications have become obsolete because of population growth. Since Oslo II, Israel has ultimately determined how much water it is willing to cede to Palestine. However, Palestine cannot succeed as a sovereign nation if it does not gain control of its own water rights, and this will likely exacerbate tensions in the region. Thus, to avoid conflict over water, Israel should consider cutting some of its own consumption and providing more to the Palestinians.

Amnesty International recently released a report [October 2009] highlighting the disparity of water consumption between Israelis and Palestinians. Israel's Ministry of Foreign Affairs reacted with indignation, asserting that Israel has exceeded the amount of water the Oslo Accords obligate it to provide the Palestinian Authority.

"While Palestinian daily water consumption barely reaches 70 litres a day per person, Israeli daily consumption is more than 300 litres per day, four times as much," Amnesty declares. The Israeli Water Authority (IWA) counters by claiming that the real averages for daily consumption are 408 liters per Israeli and 287 per Palestinian.

This isn't the first time an international organization is accusing Israel of wrongdoing over water. In the spring, the World Bank produced another study, conducted on behalf of the Palestinian Authority, that accused Israel of retarding Palestinians' development of the water resources they share with Israel, while also admonishing the Palestinians for less than stellar water management and conservation. This report faced similar recriminations from the Israeli government, charging the World Bank with taking the Palestinians' side.

In the Levant, water is the most important guarantor of a state's sovereignty, allowing it to independently direct development and provide food security for its people.

Israel Controls Water in the Region

This reaction conforms to a pattern of Israel's recent interactions with the world. Israel criticized the United Nations [April 2009] report on Gaza for its alleged pro-Palestinian, anti-Israel biases. That this is happening isn't all that interesting. Assuming Amnesty's is right, the disparity isn't surprising. Conflicts involving scarce portions of sacred space and strained supplies of civilization's staples, like water and land and energy, fail to bring out the better angels of our nature. When one side had a decided military and economic advantage over its rival, resources seldom get shared in a fair way.

In the Levant, water is the most important guarantor of a state's sovereignty, allowing it to independently direct development and provide food security for its people. For the last sixty decades, Palestinians have been trying to carve a new country from a rapidly evaporating pool of liquid sovereignty. Unfortunately for Palestinian aspirations for statehood, every groundwater resource in the West Bank and Gaza Strip sits beneath its borders with Israel. While Oslo II [Accords] in 1995 laid out allocations from the shared aquifers, the divisions have grown obsolete after 14 years of population growth. And while Israel uses the martial mechanisms of occupation to restrict Palestinian access to aquifers, it routinely flouts the limits Oslo set.

While it's contentious as any other issue in need of resolution, water relations between Israelis and Palestinians come down to numbers, not faith. There's no fixed measurement of how much Temple Mount a human being needs each day to survive. But such numbers do exist for water. The World Health Organization recommends a minimum of 100 liters. In some parts of the West Bank, like the suburbs of Hebron, Palestinian villagers and semi-nomadic Bedouin far from water infrastructure get by on as little as 15 liters of water a day, often bought at exorbitant prices from roving water tankers, that's according to the World Bank study. Without question, this dire problem deserves a solution.

Israel has its back up against a security fence when it comes to water. Since its independence, Israel has made exceptional efforts to control the region's water resources, at first necessary for the cultivation of national pride and identity through agriculture. Farming still takes the lion's share of Israel's water supplies. With economic development, population growth, and an immigration policy designed to replace Palestinian laborers with foreign hands, Israel's demand for water has risen, straining the ecological balance between human beings and their environment. Israel's reluctance to release its grasp on water resources isn't surprising.

Palestinian Petitions for More Water

The Palestinians are in even worse shape, lacking sole, sovereign control over any water resources. The Palestinian Authority shares all of its groundwater resources with Israel. The entire West Bank sits on top of three different aquifer basins, together known as the Mountain Aquifer, circumscribed by the 1949 Armistice Line. And while Hamas [the Palestinian political organization that governs the Palestinian portion of the Gaza Strip] and its rival Israel might not be on speaking terms just yet, the borders of the Gaza Strip also cross the Coastal Aquifer, another water resource Palestinians share with Israelis.

For the West Bank, a dysfunctional bureaucratic body called the Joint Water Committee (JWC) decides whether or not to approve Palestinian requests for well drilling permits. Set up under Oslo and composed of Palestinian and Israeli representatives from their respective water authorities, the JWC vetoes almost all Palestinian applications for increased access to groundwater. The Palestinians, of course, have no way to prevent Israel from drilling wells.

The Israelis . . . say that if left to their own devices, Palestinians would destroy the Mountain Aquifer by over pumping.

The Israelis, however, say that if left to their own devices, Palestinians would destroy the Mountain Aquifer by over pumping. They point to the Gaza Strip, where Palestinian over abstraction from the Coastal Aquifer has caused the sea to seep into the aquifer and render 90 percent of it saline. In answer to Palestinian demands for more wells in the West Bank, Israel offers two solutions. The first involves the construction of a desalination plant along the Mediterranean Sea, manufacturing water through an expensive energy intensive process that produces hyper-saline wastewater, dangerous to marine life if dumped back into the sea. The other option Israel proposes is building wastewater treatment and reuse plants to recycle sewage for use in agriculture, freeing up fresh, natural water for domestic and industrial purposes. Israel also criticizes the Palestinian Authority for not cracking down on unregistered [drilling] that abstracts more water than Oslo allows, most of them near Jenin and Jericho.

To desalination, the Palestinian Authority says it simply can't pay for manufactured water pumped hundreds of meters to Palestinian population centers like Nablus, a city with some of the most expensive water in the West Bank already. Furthermore, Palestinians and their advocates say that even if donor money does cut the cost of building a desalination plant, that money won't continue to flow to maintain the facility or purchase the chemicals necessary for desalination. Relying on international loans and donations to pay the water bill doesn't sound appealing either. As for wastewater treatment and reuse, Palestinian members of the JWC routinely reject Israeli proposals that couple approval of treatment plant permits with requirements that they [reuse] wastewater from settlements. Palestinians on the JWC don't want to create "facts on the ground" that legitimate the presence of Israeli settlements.

The Palestinian counter-argument is fairly simple. Israel should expand its capacity to desalinate seawater and should grant drilling rights to the Palestinian Authority. The Palestinians also argue that Israel is already set to start desalinating almost a billion cubic meters of seawater over the next decade, so there's no reason not to relinquish a share of the Mountain Aquifer to Palestinian taps. It is, after all, the only natural water resource native to Palestinian territory, while Israel controls the Sea of Galilee and its new desalination plant at Ashkelon manufactures a million cubic meters of water a year. Geography, economics, and politics deny Palestine that option.

A Contest over Water Sovereignty

But Israel objects to being obligated to depend on desalination for the Palestinians sake. And that's understandable, the Palestinians don't want to either. The real question here concerns sovereignty. Sure, if the Palestinian Authority agreed to buy desalinated water from Israel, it would receive water from Israel. But it doesn't want that water. "I wouldn't buy it for a penny," Dr. Shaddad Attili, head of the Palestinian Water Authority [PWA], said at a UN [United Nations] and PWA sponsored conference in April [2009]. What Palestinians want is the psychological assurance of sovereign, independent control over water resources.

A real Palestinian state will never emerge without a sovereign and sufficient water supply based on equitable and reasonable allocations for both sides.

Given the nature of the trans-boundary water in question, this isn't likely to happen. But a real Palestinian state will never emerge without a sovereign and sufficient water supply based on equitable and reasonable allocations for both sides. Indeed, a Palestinian country could have all the bureaucratic and coercive organs of a state, but without independent control over its water, it wouldn't be truly sovereign. Unable to direct economic development or provide for the needs of its people, such a state would probably collapse, becoming subject to its neighbors and beholden to a foreign hand on the proverbial tap.

And another grim specter looms: climate change. Over the next fifty years, studies conducted by German, Jordanian, Israeli, and Palestinian scientists point to a potential ten percent decrease in rainfall, with summertime temperatures spiking by several degrees Celsius, threatening to evaporate strained surface water sources like the Sea of Galilee. Already, 250 million cubic meters of water evaporate out of the Sea each year. The aquifers also need rainfall to recharge.

Anecdotal evidence supports these models. Israeli and Palestinian octogenarians I've spoken to agree with one thing: the weather's gotten hotter since they were kids, with much less rain. Recently, the precipitation the region does receive has come sometimes in the form of springtime torrents instead of autumn showers. More than 90 percent of Palestinian agriculture relies on rainfall, so climate change poses a real danger to that sector of the economy.

Assuming President Obama's promises to reinitiate meaningful peace negotiations come true, one of the first issues he should bring up is water.

A New International Negotiating Strategy Is Needed

So what should happen? Clearly, Washington [D.C., US capital], London [British capital], and Brussels [Belgium, capital of the European Union] need to address this issue of water publicly. There is good reason to do so. After a hopeful beginning this spring, the [Barack] Obama administration, mired in Afghanistan and brawling with Congress over health care reform, appears to have put the Israel-Palestine situation aside. Assuming President Obama's promises to reinitiate meaningful peace negotiations come true, one of the first issues he should bring up is water. An urgent issue with a quantifiable solution, a deal involving water, a politically innocuous issue to Western polities in water rich countries, could even draw passive support from the American public. It's difficult to imagine Michael Savage or Glenn Beck, two racially insensitive conservative shock jocks, marshalling caricatures of greedy

Arabs stealing water from defenseless Israel with Obama their eager accomplice. But anything's possible.

So perhaps "water for peace" could replace "land for peace" as Obama's mantra in negotiations for the next decade. From the perspective of an Israeli politician, giving more water to Palestinians would be a great bargain. Today, just two percent of Israel's GDP [gross domestic product] comes from agriculture yet the sector uses more than half the country's water. Cutting some of the kibbutzim's water subsidies would be politically painless compared to say, forcibly dismantling the city of Ariel, an Israeli settlement with its own hospital and university.

Indeed, the beauty behind allocating more water to Palestinians is that it enhances the value of the land they have left without forcing Israel to meet politically unfeasible Palestinian demands, like splitting Jerusalem. Israel's Prime Minister, Benyamin Netanyahu, has already identified Palestinian economic growth as key to Israel's security, creating jobs and distraction for otherwise unemployed, disgruntled youth.

This perspective might sound cynical, but it's just realistic. Few people in power in Washington are willing to listen to any plan for Israel-Palestine lacking the preamble: "This would be in Israel's security interest because . . ." But [it] doesn't mean improving the Palestinians' lot is impossible. Solving water is a first step no peace scheme can afford to skip, lest a "final status" solution become another indefinite "interim period." Then again, if the past serves as prologue, I wouldn't advise Obama to get his hopes up.

12

Middle Eastern Governments Must Increase Fresh Water Conservation

Jon B. Alterman and Michael Dziuban

Jon B. Alterman is director and senior fellow of the Middle East Program at the Center for Strategic & International Studies (CSIS), a public policy research institution. He teaches Middle Eastern studies at the Johns Hopkins School of Advanced International Studies and George Washington University. Michael Dziuban is a research assistant in the Middle East Program at CSIS.

Many Middle Eastern countries have unsustainable water use policies. Governments of these nations must begin reforming such policies in order to demonstrate that water is a vital resource to the region and therefore must be conserved. Governments in the region should invest in water recovery systems to catch and reuse wastewater. They also should set realistic prices for water and charge fines for those who exceed set limits. Finally, these governments should restructure the way water is used for agriculture, the sector of regional economies that consumes most of this precious resource.

Water scarcity will be important to every country in the Middle East, though it will matter in different countries in different ways. For every country, however, a combination

Jon B. Alterman and Michael Dziuban, "Clear Gold: Water as a Strategic Resource in the Middle East," CSIS.org, December 2010. Copyright © 2010 by Center for Strategic and International Studies. All rights reserved. Reproduced by permission.

87

of government action and inaction shaped existing water problems; and only government action can prevent the most negative political consequences.

Treating Wastewater and Powering Desalination Plants

On the supply side, governments trying to sustain agriculture need to investigate using treated wastewater for irrigation in order to extend the life of groundwater resources. Jordan has already had marked success on this front—about 70 percent of irrigation in the Jordan Valley now uses treated wastewater—and the UAE [United Arab Emirates] has implemented a similar change for public landscaping plots in Abu Dhabi. Using wastewater in these ways requires significant investment in sewage networks and treatment technologies that some countries may not be able to afford on their own. Yet many in the policy community consider treated wastewater a cutting-edge option for agriculture, and the examples of Jordan and the UAE suggest that the proper combination of investment and government will is within the reach of rich and poor countries alike.

There is no way that [the Middle Eastern water] supply can continue to grow indefinitely. Some constraints will have to be placed on the demand side.

Rich countries have more options for enhancing water supply, but the energy they have for desalination and water treatment is by no means infinite. Desalination fed by oil and natural gas will remain a mainstay, but countries would do well to consider alternative methods. Nuclear power production in particular creates a large amount of waste heat that can outpace the drop in electricity demand that occurs in many arid countries in the wintertime. This heat would be sufficient to fire desalination plants year-round without the need for additional energy, and could make the link between energy production and water production much more efficient. For countries whose need to provide energy will increasingly strain their ability to provide water, nuclear desalination could be an investment in the security of both of these resources and their political value.

Imposing Water Tariffs

Still, there is no way that supply can continue to grow indefinitely. Some constraints will have to be placed on the demand side. One aspect of such a change is pricing. Current patterns of water use accurately reflect the fact that water is free or nearly so, and its supplies are unlimited. Without some sort of water tariff that at least covers the economic cost of producing water—and more ideally covers the social cost of using water—it is hard to imagine that patterns of use will change much. Countries have had some success reforming water tariffs on a local level, but applying uniform tariff systems nationwide, especially across various agricultural areas, is critical. Tariff systems also have to impose decisive penalties for exceeding a certain level of water use, and government authorities have to be equally stringent in collecting bills and fines. In addition to penalties, governments could think about providing financial bonuses to individuals and companies who show promise of responsible water use and develop solid track records of conservation. Ultimately, structuring reward and punishment around resource provision is an ingrained part of politics in many Middle Eastern countries, and integrating positive incentives with more robust water tariffs could channel this established way of thinking into real water conservation.

Smart Meters Will Monitor Consumption

In concert with a tariff scheme, countries could conserve huge amounts of water by using advanced technologies for water metering. "Smart meters," which measure consumption and relay the information to a central body for monitoring and pricing, can help government authorities see how much water is being used and where, and serve as the foundation for enforcing a more robust water tariff. The UAE, which has one of the highest rates of water consumption in the world, is about two years away from having all of Abu Dhabi covered by smart meters, and about three or four years from reforming water tariffs based on the metering scheme. As other countries in the Middle East think about how to confront their water challenges, Abu Dhabi's efforts could serve as a powerful example. Many countries have the money to make such investments feasible and worthwhile, and poorer ones could perhaps make a case for donor investment to help cover the costs. For governments steeped in the view that technological advancement and control of the natural environment are hallmarks of the modern state, advanced water conservation technologies could enhance domestic security and narratives of national progress along with water supply itself.

In many [Middle Eastern] countries, agriculture makes a minor contribution to national wealth, even though it uses well over half of national water supplies.

Rethinking Agricultural Water Use

Reforming the way agriculture functions within national economies is a necessary complement to demand-side reforms. In many countries, agriculture makes a minor contribution to national wealth, even though it uses well over half of national water supplies. Prices of agricultural goods often do not reflect the amount of water required to grow them, so producers simply water, plant, and harvest as much as they can in order to maximize profits. Restructuring agricultural markets so that prices and tariffs reflect the water requirements of various crops could encourage farmers to tailor their water use to the quantities of crops the market requires, rather than the quantities they want to produce. When combined with robust water tariffs, such a shift could help maximize the value of agriculture while minimizing its water input. If water is to be used for farming, the returns on crops must be high enough to justify that use and contribute substantially to national wealth.

If water is treated as a free resource, it will continue to be treated as an inexhaustible one.

For some countries, the question of water demand for agriculture may lead to much starker conclusions about what it makes sense to use water for. Pouring upwards of 90 percent of a finite resource into transient goods such as vegetables and landscaping—as many Gulf countries do—is simply unsustainable. Future agriculture in the region will need to move to greenhouses, and much will need to move out of the region altogether. Changing the way ordinary people think about water will also be vital to generating consistent water savings and helping countries even begin to keep pace with growing populations. If water is treated as a free resource, it will continue to be treated as an inexhaustible one.

The Need to Act Quickly

These and other reforms will need to happen quickly. The Middle East is moving rapidly towards total depletion of its groundwater resources. The consequences could be unlike anything the region has seen previously, as water loss poses a new and unfamiliar challenge. It is a challenge governments have been quick to bring about and one they must be equally quick to protect themselves against.

It's wrong to assume that many Middle Eastern countries are, institutionally, not yet ripe for water reform. Certainly any reform has certain preconditions—accountability, transparency, mutual trust between rulers and subjects—that are often absent in the Middle East. Efforts to encourage water conservation and stave off political instability may encounter the frustrating reality that politics seem to need fundamental restructuring before true conservation measures can take hold.

But effective reform is still within reach if governments work as much as possible within existing political and economic structures—framing water conservation in terms that citizens can understand and rewarding it with the kinds of incentives to which they are accustomed. Innovation will be critical, but new solutions must employ the logic of existing political and social arrangements. There is no time to wait.

13

Fresh Water Access Can Present Opportunities for International Cooperation

Karin R. Bencala and Geoffrey D. Dabelko

A former program assistant at the Woodrow Wilson International Center for Scholars in Washington, D.C., Karin R. Bencala is now serving as water resources planner with the Interstate Commission on the Potomac River Basin, an organization that seeks to conserve and maintain the waterway through the cooperation of state governments. Geoffrey D. Dabelko is the director of the Environmental Change and Security Program (ECSP), a nonpartisan public policy forum at the Woodrow Wilson International Center for Scholars.

Access to fresh water has been touted as a contributor to international conflicts especially in areas with water scarcity. While not rejecting the role of water access in such conflicts, the problem is overstated. Few disputes over water have led to armed conflict, and, in truth, nations are more likely to cooperate over water access to avoid warfare. To remove the threat of international conflict over looming water shortages, politicians should focus on past efforts to peacefully resolve water access issues. Multistate agreements that apportion water rights can be used to undermine tensions, and post-conflict water concessions are a viable way to placate lingering animosity among nations. Thus, instead of emphasizing water as a source of conflict, peacemakers should capitalize on water as a tool of compromise.

Karin R. Bencala and Geoffrey D. Dabelko, "Water Wars: Obscuring Opportunities," *Journal of International Affairs*, Spring/Summer 2008. www.jia.sipa.columbia.edu. Copyright © 2008 by Journal of International Affairs. All rights reserved. Reproduced by permission.

Speaking at the 2008 World Economic Forum in Davos, Switzerland, United Nations Secretary General Ban Ki-moon weighed in on water conflict:

> The challenge of securing safe and plentiful water for all is one of the most daunting challenges faced by the world today ... Too often, where we need water, we find guns instead. Population growth will make the problem worse. So will climate change. As the global economy grows, so will its thirst. Many more conflicts lie just over the horizon.

Ban's water wars warning served to bring water to the attention of a diverse and powerful audience. Yet there is a real danger that by imprecisely stating—or overstating—the likelihood of water conflict, this argument could undercut opportunities that water offers for cooperation.

Dire Predictions Induce Global Pessimism

His prediction is not unique. We are constantly bombarded with heated predictions of coming water wars: newspaper headlines trumpet the possibility, advocates warn against it, and politicians confidently predict the next war will be over water, not oil. Truly dire statistics on declining amounts of water available for human consumption reinforce a deep pessimism over the future of water.

Evidence from systematic assessments of bilateral and multilateral interactions over water suggests a cooperative narrative is more accurate than a violent one.

Yet if we move beyond surface-level arguments, we find a decidedly more mixed story. There is considerable conflict over water, but it is not necessarily where politicians, journalists or advocates suggest we should expect it. Countries have historically been quick to rattle their sabers over water, but they have nevertheless been content to keep them sheathed.

One hears of few—if any—actual cases of wars being fought over water. Instead, evidence from systematic assessments of bilateral and multilateral interactions over water suggests a co-operative narrative is more accurate than a violent one. Successful cooperation within many transboundary river basins has become a powerful counter-story to the ubiquitous water wars prediction.

At the same time, it would be wrong to conclude that water does not precipitate conflict simply because states have not fought full-fledged wars over it in the past. If we move beyond the classic realist focus on states to analyze conflict at the subnational level, we find extensive violence surrounding water. While it does not involve armies on the move, these conflicts carry high stakes—and life and death consequences—for those involved. Conflicts over the pricing of water, large mega-projects such as dams, competing sectoral water uses and limited supplies within sectors have engendered a long record of violent, if not always large-scale or deadly, conflict.

As Ban highlighted, in the coming years, population growth, expanding agricultural production, increased consumption levels and climate change will give rise to an unprecedented scarcity of safe water. At the same time, as nations become increasingly dependent on each other for food and other goods and services, the need to cooperate will become even more imperative. Hence, the challenge for scholars and practitioners alike is to differentiate between the various dynamics that can lead to conflict over water and find ways to capitalize on the range of opportunities for cooperation.

Addressing the history of water conflict and expanding opportunities for cooperation requires that we unpack the distinctions among different levels of analysis and accompanying evidence. To do so, we delve into the historical evidence for water wars and find it absent. To the contrary, we find the case for cooperation around water to be compelling at the transboundary level. Yet within states there is considerable conflict over water. These conflicts are diverse in nature and manifestation but present a more accurate picture of water conflict. The future of transboundary water conflict may not look like the past, given the severe and deteriorating conditions for water quality and quantity, which are pushing states and peoples into unprecedented territory. Therefore, we leave open the possibility for future conflict. We conclude with an appeal for recognizing the distinctions between conflict over water and the equally strong story for cooperation as a means to capture opportunities and address threats at all levels.

Although state leaders have engaged in considerable posturing over water, they have not escalated conflicts to formal levels of war between states.

The Reality of Water Wars

Over the past two decades, scholars have undertaken extensive analyses of transboundary water-related disputes. [In a 2003 *Water Policy* article Aaron T.] Wolf, [Shira B.] Yoffe and [Mark] Giordano carried out a historical assessment of transboundary water conflicts and found that of the 1,831 state-to-state water-related events that took place between 1946 and 1999, only thirty-seven were violent, and thirty of those were between Israel and one of its neighbors prior to 1971. Fully 414 of the 507 conflictual, but not necessarily violent, cases could be classified as "rhetorical hostility." Although state leaders have engaged in considerable posturing over water, they have not escalated conflicts to formal levels of war between states. In fact, the landmark study of Wolf, Yoffe and Giordano found that water has never motivated a modern war between two nations. Where water does play a role between states, water grievances aggravate existing tensions over other issues, which can contribute to conflict.

However, water remains a conflictual resource due to its unique characteristics. Both surface water and groundwater often cross national and municipal borders. This mobility is at odds with established property rights institutions that depend on complete control of a resource. There is also no guaranteed that the same amount of water will be available from year to year; moreover, climate change models suggest that rainfall's variability will increase in the future. Nor is water easily portable like other natural resources, such as timber or fish. Finally, competing uses of water—such as agriculture, industry, energy, municipal and household use and ecosystem services—set up conflicts between sectors within and between countries. All of these characteristics make water highly contested. Yet water's interdependencies may, somewhat unexpectedly, lead more naturally to cooperation than conflict.

Coming together to manage water can offer nations with otherwise tense relationships a less threatening forum in which to make joint decisions.

The Case for Cooperation

Dire predictions of water wars attract the interest of politicians, advocates and the media, but these groups pay far less attention to the cooperation that occurs around water issues and the potential to use water as a conflict prevention and mitigation tool. Coming together to manage water can offer nations with otherwise tense relationships a less threatening forum in which to make joint decisions. The same water interdependencies among the world's 263 transboundary rivers that often make water a matter of high politics can also lead states to find ways to avoid conflict and de facto, if not proactively cooperate with one another. The fact that environmental, economic, political and security systems depend so heavily on this resource, which fluctuates in space and time, emphasizes the need for long-term, iterated coordination or cooperation.

Wolf, Yoffe and Giordano's analysis of multilateral and bilateral interactions between states bears out this counterintuitive cooperation storyline. Even as states are trading rhetorical threats, they are also engaging in a wide range of informal and formal cooperative efforts up to and including formal treaties. Wolf, Yoffe and Giordano's 2003 study found 157 instances of international water treaties. While some observers point out that the trend toward developing deeper basin integration through formal treaty mechanisms may have tapered off in recent years, the record of cooperation suggests that the water wars narrative obscures unrealized opportunities for greater efforts to capitalize on cooperation over water.

Nations have come together to form international treaties to define the general rights of upstream and downstream countries, create specific basin and waterway agreements, develop water resource management plans and conduct joint science and technology research projects.

Transboundary Agreements

Cooperation comes in many forms and over a wide variety of issues. [In a 2002 *Water Policy* article Claudia] Sadoff and [David] Grey argue that cooperation can have a variety of positive outcomes that attract potentially hostile parties to cooperation. These can be categorized as benefits to the river itself from improved ecosystem management; benefits from the river to people in the form of resources such as food; reduction of river-related costs as a result of decreased tensions; and benefits beyond the river that lead to increased cooperation and, potentially, economic payouts. Nations have come together to form international treaties to define the general rights of upstream and downstream countries, create specific basin and waterway agreements, develop water resource management plans and conduct joint science and technology research projects. These agreements frequently address the issues of equitable allocation, water quality, hydropower, natural resource use and economic development.

These international agreements are generally guided by three international water management principles that are reflected in the 1997 UN [United Nations] Convention on the Law of the Non-navigational Uses of International Watercourses: equitable and reasonable use, the avoidance of significant harm and prior notification regarding works that may affect co-riparians in transboundary watercourses. Although the UN convention has been ratified by only a handful of states and is not technically in force, these principles are increasingly becoming shared norms for transboundary water relations. They have been central to the success of transboundary efforts to turn the water wars perspective on its head.

Joint management and/or governance plans constitute other types of water cooperation that are becoming more prevalent at all political levels. One of the most often cited examples of this type of cooperation occurs along the Nile River, the impetus for many of the prominent water wars quotations from a series of Egyptian officials. The Nile Basin Initiative (NBI), a multi-year, ministerial-level negotiation among all riparians, started as a way to share scientific information among the basin countries. The initiative not only creates a forum for the joint management of the river, but also acts as a form of conflict prevention—reducing the probability that Egypt, the downstream country and regional hegemon, will force its will upon the other basin countries. Now, regional agreements over basins such as the Senegal River basin and the Niger River basin in West Africa are including the international principles of no significant harm and prior notification. International institutions such as the World Bank and the UN Development Program have been key in helping sustain these and other basin-wide and sub-basin-level negotiations.

When river basin commissions are established, a multilateral forum is created for channeling disputes and achieving greater efficiencies and development benefits.

These joint management initiatives begin by developing a shared vision for the basin. Country representatives transition from asserting their respective rights to water, to analyzing what their needs are and how water helps them meet those needs, to finally taking political boundaries off the map to identify ways to share benefits. This process also helps countries begin to meet a broad range of fundamental development needs, thereby serving as a de facto conflict prevention tool. This evolution from a unilateral, zero-sum assertion of rights to a positive-sum cooperative resource maximization strategy can provide greater benefits, reduce grievances and increase confidence among riparians. When river basin commissions are established, a multilateral forum is created for channeling disputes and achieving greater efficiencies and development benefits.

The NBI is representative of water cooperation that helps prevent interstate conflict. This is just one of four ways water cooperation can be critical to overcoming conflict. It can also serve as a lifeline for dialogue among parties in active conflict with one another. Jordan and Israel met to coordinate water management through decades of open war in the so-called "picnic table" talks. These technical-level efforts established patterns of cooperation and trust that positively contributed to larger peace negotiations and the 1994 peace deal between the two countries. The nongovernmental organization (NGO) Friends of the Earth Middle East continues this tradition at the community level with its Good Water Neighbors program, which pairs Palestinian and Israeli, and Jordanian and Israeli, communities with mutual water and sanitation dependencies. Water and sanitation investments are pitched as providing peace dividends in addition to quality-of-life improvements, increasing the potential benefits of often-expensive infrastructure projects.

Water as Peacemaker

Water cooperation can also support efforts to terminate conflict. During times of conflict, water can be a highly contested arena for negotiation even though it was not a proximate cause of the conflict. For instance, despite the presence of the 1960 Indus Waters Treaty, water is still a highly contested issue between India and Pakistan. Yet it pales in comparison to far more incendiary issues such as the status of Kashmir or perceived religious differences between Hindus and Muslims. Consequently, water has been a special focus in the bilateral negotiations between India and Pakistan, just as it has been between Palestinians and Israelis. Water may not have caused these conflicts, but the parties must begin resolving their water issues if they are to reach a sustainable peace.

Access to safe water is essential in post-conflict settings, as it is key to restarting economic activity, providing livelihoods, improving human health and strengthening the perceived legitimacy of the fledgling peace.

Finally, successful water management can prevent reignition of conflict in the early stages of post-conflict peace. Access to safe water is essential in post-conflict settings, as it is key to restarting economic activity, providing livelihoods, improving human health and strengthening the perceived legitimacy of the fledgling peace. The inability to provide water-related services in the initial months and years following the cessation of hostilities can undercut support for the terms of the peace, creating or extending perceived grievances against the state or occupying forces. Support for Iraq's national government and coalition forces has been undercut by the slow pace of improving water-related services in Iraq, which were not prioritized in the immediate aftermath of the first phase of fighting. Insurgents have regularly targeted subsequent efforts at building centralized water infrastructure. The practical, on-the-ground experiences of humanitarian NGOs and the wider analyses of post-conflict settings by the UN Environment Program's Post-Conflict and Disaster Management Branch have built a case for viewing natural resources like water as essential to restarting livelihoods and building sustainable peace.

These examples of the different roles for cooperative water management illustrate how cooperation can directly benefit peacemaking, peacekeeping and peacebuilding. It can also play a fundamental role in building trust and confidence among potential, current or former adversaries. While it is rarely stated explicitly that a project is a water conflict prevention project, these efforts often produce peace dividends in addition to water management benefits. The peacemaking goals of water management often remain unstated—as with the NBI—to keep the process less politicized and therefore more effective. Making the security goals explicit brings the more contentious security actors into the process earlier, before long-term interactions have had time to build trust between technical, non-security ministries and individuals. Exchanges between technocratic water managers, both governmental and nongovernmental, have therefore commonly preceded more political and more senior negotiations.

Organizations to Contact

The editors have compiled the following list of organizations concerned with the issues debated in this book. The descriptions are derived from materials provided by the organizations. All have publications or information available for interested readers. The list was compiled on the date of publication of the present volume; the information provided here may change. Be aware that many organizations take several weeks or longer to respond to inquiries, so allow as much time as possible.

Global Health & Education Foundation (GHEF)

3820 Blackhawk Rd., Danville, CA   94506
(877) 378-3839, (925) 736-8234 • fax: (925) 648-0163
e-mail: info@ghefoundation.org
website: www.ghefoundation.org

GHEF works to end poverty worldwide by focusing on finding solutions to problems such as disability, access to water and sanitation, disease prevention and health care, and education. One of the main projects of the organization is the Safe Drinking Water Project, in which the GHEF works alongside Chinese organizations to ensure access to safe drinking water in rural China by establishing localized water purification systems. The foundation also helped to establish the website www.drinking-water.org to provide an overview of the water access issue.

Global Rainwater Harvesting Collective

Tilonia-305816, Madan Ganj, Via Ajmer District
Rajasthan
 India
e-mail: bunkerl945@gmail.com
website: www.globalrainwaterharvesting.org

The Global Rainwater Harvesting Collective seeks to employ traditional solutions to sustainable water collection by looking to historical means of self-sufficiency and eco-sensitivity as the basis for current models of development. The organization's website provides information about ongoing and past projects that have already helped individuals who previously lacked access to water gain a sustainable supply. A case study as well as a do-it-yourself manual as to how to employ this technique can be found online.

IRC International Water and Sanitation Centre (IRC)
PO Box 82327, 2508 EH, The Hague
  The Netherlands
+31 70 304 4000 • fax: +31 70 304 4044
website: www.irc.nl

IRC has worked since its founding in 1968 to provide information to all governments, professionals, and organizations concerned with access to and sanitation of water for impoverished people living in developing countries around the world. In accordance with these goals, the organization has established regional programs worldwide to address localized water access and sanitation issues, including the Sanitation, Hygiene, and Water (SHAW) project in Indonesia, the Pan-Africa Programme, and Sanitation and Water for All. The IRC's digital library provides access to reports, books, and DVDs about water, sanitation, and hygiene issues.

Pacific Institute
654 13th St., Preservation Park, Oakland, CA   94612
(510) 251-1600 • fax: (510) 251-2203
e-mail: info@pacinst.org
website: www.pacinst.org

The Pacific Institute was founded with the goal of meeting the basic needs of all people by maintaining a healthy planet and creating sustainable communities. The organization seeks to achieve these goals through its research-based programs that seek to find solutions to problems such as water shortages and environmental degradation. It aims to educate the public and decisionmakers about the need to implement the necessary policies to address these issues. The World's Water website, www.worldwater.org, provides information about the institute's current projects as well as water data and information about the link between access to water and conflict. Water efficiency, water privatization, and bottled water are additional issues addressed on the Pacific Institute's website.

United Nations (UN)
140 E 45th St., New York, NY   10017
(212) 415-4000
website: www.un.org

The UN is an international organization composed of member nations from around the globe. It was founded in 1945, following World War II with the goal of securing international peace, fostering cooperation and dialogue among nations, improving the living standards, and ensuring the human rights of people worldwide. In accordance with these goals, the UN has focused much attention on implementing programs through its various agencies that seek to guarantee access to fresh water for all humans. The United Nations Environment Program (UNEP) published the report "Water Policy and Strategy of UNEP" outlining the organization's goals and activities regarding freshwater access. The UN also organized the International Decade for Action, Water for Life 2005–2015 to raise awareness about the issue and promote action at an international level. The website for this project offers access to a range of publications discussing water issues both generally and in specific countries and regions of the world. Additionally, the UN Water Portal, www.unwater.org, provides a centralized site for information relating to UN water-related projects and research.

US Environmental Protection Agency (EPA)
Office of Water (4100T), 1200 Pennsylvania Ave. NW
Washington, DC   20460
website: www.epa.gov

The EPA is the US governmental agency responsible for protecting human health and the environment. As such, it works to establish and implement the regulatory framework that guides states in creating localized standards to maintain the safety of their citizens. The agency also works to ensure that corporations comply with these regulations. Within the EPA, the Office of Ground Water and Drinking Water is specifically charged with tackling issues related to the provision of fresh water for all Americans. The office's website provides extensive information on drinking water protection, standards and risk management, water security, water infrastructure, and pollution prevention and control, among other topics.

Water for People
6666 W Quincy Ave., Denver, CO   80235
(720) 488-4590
e-mail: info@waterforpeople.org
website: www.waterforpeople.org

Water for People works to aid the millions of people without safe drinking water and the billions of people who lack satisfactory sanitation facilities by promoting the development of localized programs that help to build access to these necessities. The organization has projects in eleven countries: Uganda, Rwanda, Malawi, India, Honduras, Guatemala, Nicaragua, the Dominican Republic, Bolivia, Peru, and Ecuador, with information about each specific country's project available on the Water for People website. The Water for People FLOW (Field Level Operations Watch) site allows visitors an interactive look at the work the organization is doing and the current levels of service within project areas.

Water Science & Technology Board
The National Academies, 500 Fifth St. NW, Keck 607
Washington, DC   20001
(202) 334-3422 • fax: (202) 334-1961
website: http://dels.nas.edu/wstb/

The Water Science & Technology Board, a division of the National Academy of Sciences and the National Academy of Engineering, is dedicated to advancing scientific and technological knowledge necessary to improve the management and utilization of water resources around the world. The board publishes biennial reports on the status of water access and related technologies. Additionally, it maintains the water information center site, which provides comprehensive information on water-related issues such as water supply and sanitation, water quality in the natural environment, drinking water basics, and water in developing nations. Reports such as "Drinking Water: Understanding the Science and Policy Behind a Critical Resource," are available online.

WaterAid

Supporter Services, 47–49 Durham St., London SE11 5JD
   United Kingdom
+44 (0) 20 7793 4594 • fax: +44 (0) 20 7793 4545
website: www.wateraid.org

WaterAid envisions a world where no one lacks access to fresh water and sanitation. Through its work with poor people around the world, this organization seeks to help these individuals secure a steady supply of fresh water and means of hygiene, two steps the organizations sees as central to improving health, education, and livelihood, which in turn will help them to overcome poverty. WaterAid reports such as, "The Sanitation Problem: What Can and Should the Health Sector Do?" "Sanitation Framework," and "A Human Rights Based Approach to Water and Sanitation" can all be read online.

World Bank

1818 H St. NW, Washington, DC   20433
(202) 473-1000 • fax: (202) 477-6391
website: www.worldbank.org

An international, nongovernmental organization, the World Bank seeks to eradicate poverty around the world by providing both financial and technical aid to developing countries. Low interest loans are given to countries to assist in a range of areas including education, health, and environmental and natural resource management, among others. One issue central to these larger topics is access to fresh water, and the

World Bank's site on water, www.worldbank.org/water, offers comprehensive information about the organization's projects, research, and impact on this issue.

World Health Organization (WHO)
Avenue Appia 20, Geneva 27   1211
  Switzerland
+41 22 791 2111 • fax: +41 22 791 3111
e-mail: info@who.int
website: www.who.int

WHO is the agency within the United Nations charged with directing and coordinating health-related projects. It serves as a global leader in the international dialogue on how to address issues of concern, researches and promotes and publishes research on topics necessitating public concern, offers policy options, sets norms and standards of health, and monitors global health trends. The Water Sanitation and Health arm of the organization explores the connections between access to water and health and examines possible courses of action that could improve individuals' situations worldwide. Topics of focus include drinking water quality, bathing waters, water resources, and wastewater use, among others with information available on the WHO website.

Bibliography

Books

Maude Barlow — *Blue Covenant: The Global Water Crisis and the Coming Battle for the Right to Water.* New York: New Press, 2007.

Cynthia Barnett — *Blue Revolution: Unmaking America's Water Crisis.* Boston: Beacon, 2011.

Cynthia Barnett — *Mirage: Florida and the Vanishing Water of the Eastern U.S.* Ann Arbor, MI: University of Michigan Press, 2007.

Maggie Black and Jannet King — *The Atlas of Water: Mapping the World's Most Critical Resource,* Second Ed. Berkeley, CA: University of California Press, 2009.

Marq de Villiers — *Water: The Fate of Our Most Precious Resource.* New York: Mariner, 2001.

Brian Fagan — *Elixir: A History of Water and Humankind.* New York: Bloomsbury, 2011.

Charles Fishman — *The Big Thirst: The Secret Life and Turbulent Future of Water.* New York: Free Press, 2011.

Robert Glennon — *Unquenchable: America's Water Crisis and What to Do About It.* Washington, DC: Island, 2009.

Fred Pearce   *When the Rivers Run Dry: Water—The Defining Crisis of the Twenty-First Century.* Boston: Beacon, 2006.

Alex Prud'homme   *The Ripple Effect: The Fate of Fresh Water in the Twenty-First Century.* New York: Scribner, 2011.

Vandana Shiva   *Water Wars: Privatization, Pollution, and Profit.* Cambridge, MA: South End, 2002.

Steven Solomon   *Water: The Epic Struggle for Wealth, Power, and Civilization.* New York: HarperCollins, 2011.

Periodicals and Internet Sources

Rhodante Ahlers   "Fixing and Nixing: The Politics of Water Privatization," *Review of Radical Political Economics*, Spring 2010.

Maude Barlow   "The Growing Movement to Protect the Global Water Commons," *Brown Journal of World Affairs*, Fall/Winter 2010.

Economist   "Streams of Blood, or Streams of Peace," May 3, 2008. www.economist .com.

Harald D. Frederiksen   "The World Water Crisis and International Security," *Middle East Policy*, Winter 2009.

Ryan Gallagher et al.
"Water, Sustainability, and Self-Reliance," *Civil Engineering*, November 2009.

Erica Gies
"Water Wars: Is Water a Human Right or a Commodity?" *World Watch*, March/April 2009.

Andrew C. Godlewki
"'Damming' the Peace Process: Water Politics and Its Impact on the Israeli-Palestinian Conflict," *Journal of Muslim Minority Affairs*, June 2010.

Anne Harris
"Moving Ice," *Engineering & Technology*, June 2011.

Rebecca H. Hiers
"Water: A Human Right or a Human Responsibility?" *Willamette Law Review*, Spring 2011.

Arjun Kumar Khadka
"The Emergence of Water as a 'Human Right' on the World Stage: Challenges and Opportunities," *International Journal of Water Resources Development*, March 2010.

Barbara Kingsolver
"Fresh Water," *National Geographic*, April 2010.

Nicholas Köhler
"Turning Water into Money," *Maclean's*, July 11, 2011.

Thomas M. Kostigen
"Virtual Water—A Smarter Way to Think About How Much H2O You Use," *Discover*, June 2008. www .discovermagazine.com.

Beth Kowitt and Kim Thai — "The Future of Water," *Fortune*, October 12, 2009.

Upmanu Lall et al. — "Water in the 21st Century: Defining the Elements of Global Crises and Potential Solutions," *Journal of International Affairs*, Spring/Summer 2008.

Barry S. Levy and Victor W. Sidel — "Water Rights and Water Fights: Preventing and Resolving Conflicts Before They Boil Over," *American Journal of Public Health*, May 2011.

Tina Rosenberg — "The Burden of Thirst," *National Geographic*, April 2010.

Vaclav Smil — "Water News: Bad, Good and Virtual," *American Scientist*, September/October 2008. www.americanscientist.org.

Michael Totty — "High-Tech Cures for Water Shortages," *Wall Street Journal*, October 18, 2010.

Chaoqing Yu — "China's Water Crisis Needs More Than Words," *Nature*, February 17, 2011. www.nature.com.

Sarah Zielinski — "Running Dry," *Smithsonian*, October 2010. www.smithsonianmag.com.

Index